Mallorca

by Tony Kelly

Tony Kelly first visited Mallorca on a
walking holiday in 1995 and he has been
returning to the island ever since. In 2000 he
was awarded a diploma by the Mallorca
Tourist Board for his writing 'reflecting the
true spirit and diverse nature of Mallorca'.
An expert on Spain, his other guidebooks
include *AA Essential Menorca, Essential
Costa Brava* and *Spiral Gran Canaria*.
He lives near Cambridge with his wife
and young son.

Above: *Cala Sant Vicenç*

AA Publishing

Above: *Catalina Thomas,
patron saint of Mallorca,
depicted on a tile set on
the side of a house in her
home town of Valldemossa*

Written by Tony Kelly

First published 1998. Reprinted November 1998.
Second edition January 2000. Reprinted Feb, Apr, Aug and
Oct 2000, May 2001.
Reprinted April 2002. Information verified and updated.
Reprinted Aug 2002. Reprinted Jun 2003.
Information verified and updated 2004.
This edition 2005. Information verified and updated.
Reprinted May, Nov 2005.

© Automobile Association Developments Limited 2002,
2005

Published by AA Publishing, a trading name of Automobile
Association Developments Limited, whose registered
office is Fanum House, Basing View, Basingstoke,
Hampshire RG21 4EA. Registered number 1878835.

Automobile Association Developments Limited retains the
copyright in the original edition © 1998 and all subsequent
editions, reprints and amendments.

A CIP catalogue record for this book is available from the
British Library.

Find out more about
AA Publishing and the
wide range of travel
publications and services
the AA provides by
visiting our website at
www.theAA.com/
bookshop

A02865

Colour separation: BTB Digital Imaging Limited,
Whitchurch, Hampshire

Printed and bound in Italy by Printer Trento S.r.l.

Contents

About this Book

KEY TO SYMBOLS

➕ map reference to the maps found in the What to See section (see below)

✉ address or location

☎ telephone number

🕐 opening times

🍴 restaurant or café on premises or near by

Ⓜ nearest underground train station

🚌 nearest bus/tram route

🚃 nearest overground train station

🛥 ferry crossings and excursions by boat

✈ travel by air

ℹ tourist information

♿ facilities for visitors with disabilities

✋ admission charge

↔ other places of interest near by

❓ other practical information

➤ indicates the page where you will find a fuller description

---

This book is divided into five sections to cover the most important aspects of your visit to Mallorca.

Viewing Mallorca pages 5–14
An introduction to Mallorca by the author.
Mallorca's Features
Essence of Mallorca
The Shaping of Mallorca
Peace and Quiet
Mallorca's Famous

Top Ten pages 15–26
The author's choice of the Top Ten places to visit in Mallorca, with practical information.

What to See pages 27–90
Alphabetical listings of the main attractions in Palma and around the island.
Practical information
Snippets of 'Did You Know…' information
4 suggested walks
4 suggested tours
2 features

Where To... pages 91–116
Detailed listings of the best places to eat, stay, shop, take the children and be entertained.

Practical Matters pages 117–24
A highly visual section containing essential travel information.

Maps
All map references are to the individual maps in the What to See section of this guide. For example, La Seu in Palma has the reference ➕ 34B2 – indicating the page on which the map is located and the grid square in which the cathedral is to be found. A list of the maps that have been used in this travel guide can be found in the index. As with the maps, place names in the text are given in Catalan; where a Spanish word or phrase is more widely used, that is given instead.

Prices
Where appropriate, an indication of the cost of an establishment is given by € signs: €€€ denotes higher prices, €€ denotes average prices, while € denotes lower charges.

Star Ratings
Most of the places described in this book have been given a separate rating:
✪✪✪   Do not miss
✪✪ Highly recommended
✪   Worth seeing

Viewing
Mallorca

Above: *Green shutters,
Cala Santanyí;*
Right: *Old timer in local
café in Muro*

Tony Kelly's Mallorca

Mallorca or Majorca?
Are they the same place or not? Yes and no. Majorca, with a hard 'j', is a place invented by foreigners, where the sun always shines, the beer flows and the nearest you get to local culture is an argument with a taxi-driver. Mallorca, the local name for the island, is somewhere quite different and far more complex. This book is about Mallorca.

Sheep with bells around their necks grazing beneath olive trees; hilltop sanctuaries where you spend the night in what was once a monk's cell. These are probably not your typical images of Mallorca.

If you thought Mallorca was all sweaty bodies, in the disco and on the beach, think again. It is that, of course – that's the main reason why 8 million tourists visit the island every year. But there is an awful lot more to Mallorca than sun, sea and sand.

Whisper it gently, but Mallorca is changing its image. Fed up with being labelled cheap and cheerful, it has gone for a new approach. High-rise apartment blocks are being torn down, to be replaced by tree-lined promenades. Manor houses and country estates are being converted into stylish hotels. Tourists are encouraged to come in winter, to walk, cycle and play golf. The island that led the way into mass tourism is now leading the way out.

Not just sand and sea – Mallorca is starting to attract walkers and cyclists

For such a small island, the variations are extraordinary. You can spend one day lying on the beach, the next walking in the mountains. Castles, caves, countryside, hidden coves... whatever you want from a holiday, it is probably there. Except, perhaps, snow.

Of course there is nowhere in Mallorca still waiting to be 'discovered' – even the tiniest villages are heavily dependent on tourism. But strike off the main roads and into the small towns on the plain, simply go wherever you see a cluster of brown houses on a hill, and you will find a Mallorca utterly at odds with the familiar image.

Mallorca's Features

Geography
• Mallorca is the largest of the Balearic islands, a group that includes Menorca, Ibiza and Formentera.
• Mallorca measures 100km from east to west and 75km from north to south.
• Mallorca lies 200km south of Barcelona off the east coast of Spain.
• Mallorca has 555km of coastline and 80 beaches.
• The rocky islands Cabrera and Sa Dragonera provide havens for nesting seabirds.
• The Serra de Tramuntana and Serra de Llevant are two mountain ranges divided by a fertile central plain.
• Palma has an average daily maximum temperature of 21.4°C and an average of seven hours of sunshine per day throughout the year.

Pine-clad cliffs lean into the sea along the spectacular north coast

Tourism
• Mallorca received 1 million tourists in 1966, 3 million in 1978 and 8 million in 2000, of whom 41% were from Germany, 26% from Britain and 12% from Spain.
• On busy days in summer up to 700 flights land at Palma airport, carrying up to 100,000 passengers.
• Mallorca has 200,000 hotel beds and 60,000 in tourist apartments.
• Mallorca has enough restaurant tables for a quarter of the population to eat out every night.
• Mallorca's GDP (Gross Domestic Product) per capita is more than 50% above the Spanish average. Two thirds of the population work in tourism, which represents about 60% of GDP.

Language
• The official languages are Catalan and Castilian Spanish, though Catalan has enjoyed a strong revival in recent years and is now the preferred language in education and local government.
• Most people speak Mallorquín, a dialect of Catalan.

People
Of 700,000 people in Mallorca, half live in the capital Palma. The next biggest towns are Manacor (35,000) and Inca (25,000). The population has doubled since 1950 and includes a large number of expatriates – mostly German and British.

7

Essence of Mallorca

Mallorca's character is shaped, above all, by its climate. The people of the Mediterranean know how to take life slowly – they still have time to sit in the shade and chat, to take a siesta rather than rushing back to work, to enjoy the outdoors whether it is the mountains or the sea.

The warm climate has long attracted outsiders, whose influence can still be felt; Romans, Arabs and Europeans have all left their mark on Mallorca's landscape and culture. But what have not changed are the enduring values of an island people, courteous, proud and self-sufficient.

Aquarium at Porto Cristo (above); fisherman at Port de Sóller (below); the dubious attractions of Platja de Palma (right)

THE **10** ESSENTIALS

*If you only have a short time to visit Mallorca,
or would like to get a real flavour of the island,
here are the essentials:*

• **Spend a day in Palma**
exploring the old city, then
join the evening *passeig*
along the waterfront for a
drink in one of the island's
trendiest bars (➤ 30–40).
• **Take the joyride to Sóller**
on a vintage electric train
through the mountains
(➤ 71).
• **Enjoy a boat trip** around
the coast, passing hidden
coves which you cannot
reach in a car.
• **Walk in the Serra de
Tramuntana** (➤ 83–4),
breathing in the heady mix of
fresh air, sea breeze and
scented wild herbs.
• **Sit at a quayside
restaurant** eating fresh fish –
choose from any one of the
island's ports (➤ 92–9).

*Take the tram to Port de
Sóller and the boat to Sa
Calobra – or spend the
day working on your tan*

• **Visit the monastery at
Valldemossa** where Chopin
and George Sand spent the
winter of 1838–39 (➤ 26).
• **Drive (or walk) to a hilltop
sanctuary** to experience 'the
other Mallorca' – if you really
want to get away from it all,
spend the night.
• **Visit the traditional
market at Sineu** (➤ 86) to
haggle over everything from
sausages to sheep.
• **Brave the crowds on a
resort beach** – you haven't
'done' Mallorca until you have.
• **Find out where there is a
local festival going on**
(➤ 116) – and drop
everything to get there.

The Shaping of Mallorca

5000 BC
Evidence of human habitation in caves on the north coast.

1300–800 BC
The Talaiotic culture creates settlements like those at Artà and Capocorb Vell.

400 BC
First references to *honderos* (Balearic slingers) fighting in the Punic Wars.

123 BC
The island is conquered by the Romans, who name it Balearis Major, introduce vineyards and olives, and establish their capital at Pollentia, now Alcúdia.

AD 426
Vandal invasion leads to the persecution of Christians.

534
Byzantine conquest restores Christianity and brings Mallorca into the province of Sardinia.

902
Arab invasion – Mallorca enters the Caliphate of Córdoba. Oranges and almonds are introduced, along with windmills and irrigation techniques. Palma, known as Medina Mayurqa, is the envy of Europe, with street lights and heated baths.

1229
The origins of modern Mallorca – the conquest by Jaume I of Aragón. Catalan becomes the main language.

1275
Ramón Llull establishes his first hermitage at Puig de Randa.

1276
On Jaume I's death, his kingdom is divided up and his son Jaume II becomes the first King of Mallorca.

1276–1349
The 'Golden Age of Independence' – the building of Castell de Bellver, Palau de l'Almudaina and Alcúdia's city walls.

1349
Jaume III is killed at Llucmajor and Mallorca's independence ends when the island is reincorporated into Aragón.

1492
Modern Spain is created with the union of Aragón, Castile and Granada.

16th–18th Centuries
Repeated pirate attacks lead to the building of watchtowers around the coast.

1715
After victory in the War of the Spanish Succession, Felipe V imposes central rule and the Castilian language on the island of Mallorca.

Statue of Ramón Llull on the waterfront at Palma

1836
Opening of a steamer service between Mallorca and Spain.

1879–98
Period of 'gold fever' due to the booming export trade in wine and almonds – until the vines are destroyed by the phylloxera virus, leading to mass emigration.

1902–3
The Gran Hotel opens in Palma. Thomas Cook runs its first tours to Mallorca.

1905
Founding of the Fomento del Turismo de Mallorca (tourist board).

1929
Opening of the Hotel Formentor.

1936–39
The Spanish Civil War, followed by dictatorship under General Franco.

1950
The first charter flight lands in Mallorca.

1960
The opening of Son Sant Joan airport leads to the start of the tourist boom.

1966
Mallorca receives one million tourists.

The Spanish Civil War led to repression throughout Spain

1975
Death of Franco and restoration of the monarchy.

1978
A new constitution grants limited autonomy to the Spanish regions.

1983
The Balearic Islands become an autonomous region with their capital at Palma. Catalan becomes the official language.

1984
Opening of La Residencia hotel in Deià.

1986
Spain joins the European Community.

1988
A new coastal law prohibits further development within 100m of the sea.

1997
The new terminal at Son Sant Joan airport is launched, increasing capacity to 27 million passengers a year.

2002
An 'ecotax' on tourists is introduced – and dropped in 2003.

Peace & Quiet

Olive trees near Andratx – it is still surprisingly easy to get away from it all in Mallorca

If you want peace and quiet in Mallorca, go in winter – only 10 per cent of foreign tourists visit between November and March. The island is particularly beautiful in February, when almond blossom carpets the ground like snow. Even in the height of summer, there are plenty of opportunities to escape the crowds. Half of the locals live in Palma, and 90 per cent of the tourists stay on a few small stretches of coast – which leaves large areas of Mallorca just waiting to be explored.

Rights of Way

Walkers have the right of way on all coastal paths, plus routes to miradors, monasteries and mountain peaks (except Puig Major). In recent years, many landowners have attempted to deny access by erecting 'private' signs. If challenged, just state clearly where you are going.

Walking

The obvious areas are the mountains, especially the Serra de Tramuntana (▶ 83–84). At the lower levels, up to around 700m, you walk through *garrigue*, a typical Mediterranean landscape where Aleppo pines mix with wild olives and the stony ground sprouts beautiful wild flowers – orchids and peonies and cistus and asphodel – in spring. (Spring here arrives early, from late February through to May.) Higher up, you reach the *maquis* scrubland, where little grows apart from thorny bushes of heather, bracken, rosemary and broom. Above 1,000m the land is barren – but the views from this height are magnificent and the sense of isolation complete.

Take sensible precautions when walking in the mountains – good boots, extra clothing, food and water, a map, compass and whistle. If you prefer more gentle walks, just strike out along any of the minor roads between the small towns on the plain, or follow a coastal footpath to find your own private bay.

Birds

Mallorca is a paradise for birdwatchers, who come from all over Europe each spring and autumn to see migrating birds on their way to and from wintering in Africa. The best times are April to May and September to October, and the best areas are S'Albufera (▶ 77) and the Salines de Llevant near Ses Salines (▶ 85). The reedbeds of S'Albufera come alive each spring with the song of herons and warblers; other species include egrets, terns, hoopoes, sandpipers and woodcat shrike. Numerous wading birds and wildfowl are attracted to the salt marshes at Ses Salines, including plovers, stilts, water rails and black-tailed godwits. Good spots for watching seabirds include Cap de Ses Salines on the south coast and Cap de Formentor in the northeast (▶ 18), where shags and shearwaters nestle on the cliffs.

Birds of Prey

The mountains of the Serra de Tramuntana are a haven for birds of prey, including ospreys, peregrines, Montagu's harriers and Eleanora's falcons. Rarest of all are the black vultures, of which only a few dozen remain in the area around Lluc monastery. An exhibition at the monastery describes a conservation programme to protect both these and another endangered species, the Mallorcan midwife toad. The best places to see black vultures, and other predatory birds, are at the Cúber and Gorg Blau reservoirs on the road through the mountains from Lluc to Sóller.

The mountain ranges of Mallorca are one of the last remaining European habitats of the black vulture

Mallorca's Famous

Michael Douglas (1944–)
The American actor Michael Douglas is a frequent visitor to Mallorca, where he has a home overlooking the north coast. His passion for Mallorca is reflected in the Costa Nord cultural centre (➤ 51) in Valldemossa, which he founded in 2000. In 2003, he was appointed as a roving tourism ambassador for the Balearic Islands.

Ramón Llull

Ramón Llull (1235–1316) was a wealthy courtier in Palma until a disastrous seduction attempt (➤ 75) led him to retire to Puig de Randa in isolation. Devoting himself to prayer and study, he wrote in Catalan and Latin on everything from algebra to metaphysics; he is widely seen as the father of the Catalan language. Recalled to the court by Jaume II, he established an Oriental language school at Valldemossa and learnt Arabic with the help of a Moorish slave. He was stoned to death attempting to convert Muslims in Tunisia.

Junípero Serra

The Mallorcan missionary Junípero Serra (1713–84) is honoured in the Capitol in Washington as 'the founder of California'. Of course California was there already; but it was Serra, sent there at the age of 54 after 14 years in Mexico, who established the missions which have grown into some of America's biggest cities, including San Diego and San Francisco. A museum in his home town of Petra (➤ 64) tells the story. He was beatified in 1988, the first step on the road to sainthood.

Joan Miró

Though not strictly Mallorcan, Joan Miró (1893–1983), the Catalan artist, spent the last 27 years of his life in Mallorca and the islanders have adopted him as their own. His bright, surreal designs adorn everything from tourist posters (the widely used España and Mallorca logos are his) to T-shirts and the mural in the Parc de la Mar in Palma. His house and studio near Palma have been turned into a gallery of his work (➤ 56).

Statue of Junípero Serra in Palma (above); Joan Miró at work (right)

Top Ten

Above: *Narrow streets of
Valldemossa;*
Right: *Detail on Portal del Mirador,
La Seu*

1
Alcúdia

 29D5

 Choice of restaurants and bars (€–€€)

From Palma/Port d'Alcúdia

Port d'Alcúdia (➤ 67)

Market held Tue, Sun

Ciutat Romà

 Tue–Fri 10–4, Sat–Sun 10–1

Cheap

Museu Monogràfic de Pollentia

 Carrer Sant Jaume 30

971 547004

 Tue–Fri 10–4, Sat–Sun 10–1

Joint entry with Ciutat Romà

Portal del Moll leads directly into the heart of the city

A perfectly restored walled city on the site of a Roman settlement, with remains of Roman houses and an amphitheatre.

Not to be confused with the holiday resort of the same name, which is actually down at Port d'Alcúdia (➤ 67), the old town is a gem of a place, a maze of narrow streets enclosed by carefully restored medieval ramparts. There were Phoenician and Greek settlements here, but the town reached its heyday in the 2nd century BC, when the Roman invaders made it their capital, Pollentia ('power'). Destroyed by Vandals in the 6th century, the town returned to greatness under the Moors, who built *al-kudia* ('the town on the hill'). The walls you see today were added after the Spanish conquest in the 14th century.

You enter the city through one of the two town gates – the Portal del Moll, with two square towers and two palm trees standing guard, is the symbol of Alcúdia. The narrow streets of the old town, especially Carrer d'en Serra, are resonant of Palma's Arab quarter.

A short walk from the parish church of Sant Jaume takes you to three interesting sights, connected by signposted footpaths. Closest to town are the remains of Roman houses at Pollentia, **Ciutat Romà**; near here are the well-preserved Teatre Romà (Roman amphitheatre) and the Oratori de Santa Anna, one of Mallorca's oldest churches. After exploring the Roman remains, interpret them at the **Museu Monogràfic de Pollentia** beside the parish church.

2
Badia de Palma
(Palma Bay)

*The good, the bad and the ugly sides
of Mallorca's tourist development meet along
a 25-km stretch of coast.*

The former villages of S'Arenal and Magaluf sit facing each other across Palma Bay. Once upon a time, a fisherman casting his net into the sea at S'Arenal could have gazed around an empty coastline where the only buildings to stand out would have been Palma's cathedral and castle. Nowadays he would barely be able to distinguish them among a continuous stretch of hotels, a concrete jungle extending all the way to Magaluf. And he wouldn't be there anyway as there are few fish left to catch.

Like it or loathe it, you are bound to spend some time in Palma Bay – even if you are not staying here, you should visit at least once to see some of the best, and the worst, that Mallorca has to offer. Each of the

✚ 28B3

🍴 Numerous bars and restaurants in all the resorts (€)

🚌 From Palma to all the resorts

resorts (described separately in the What To See section) has its own character – young or old, British or German, cheap and cheerful or jet-set rich. One moment you can be in Portals Nous, with its chic marina crammed with millionaires' yachts (you have to be seriously rich just to look at the restaurant menus here), the next in seedy Magaluf, all British pubs and wet T-shirt contests.

Occasionally you come across a glimpse of what this coastline must once have been like. Follow the road beyond Magaluf through the pine woods. Suddenly you are among tiny coves where, out of season, you might still find your own private beach. Eventually you reach the headland of Cap de Cala Figuera where you can look back at sweeping views of the entire bay. Cliffs plunge into the clear blue sea, with not a hotel in sight. Come up here at midnight for utter peace and solitude; but listen carefully and you might just be able to hear the disco beat of Magaluf pounding away beneath you.

Boat tours of Palma Bay in summer from Palma, S'Arenal, Palma Nova and Magaluf

♿ Level beach promenades at Platja de Palma and Magaluf

↔ Magaluf (► 59), Palma Nova (► 63), Platja de Palma (► 64), Portals Nous (► 72), Portals Vells (► 72), Ses Illetes (► 85)

Sun, sea and sand but little solitude – resorts like Magaluf epitomise the growth of Mallorcan tourism

17

3
Cap de Formentor

✚ 29E5

🍴 Café with snacks at Cap de Formentor (€); restaurant (€€€) in Hotel Formentor

🚌 From Palma and Port de Pollença in summer

⛴ From Port de Pollença to Formentor beach and Cap de Formentor in summer

❓ The best time to see birds and flowers is spring

There are several opportunities to stop and admire the view along the twisting road to Cap de Formentor

This wild peninsula on Mallorca's northeast tip has stunning views, sandy beaches and the island's original luxury hotel.

The 20-km drive from Port de Pollença to Mallorca's most northerly point has scenery as dramatic as anyone could wish for. Cliffs 400m tall jut into the sea, their weird rock formations attracting nesting seabirds, while pine trees seem to grow out of the rocks. The drive is also famously scary – a local legend has it that the parish priest and the local bus driver arrived at the Pearly Gates, and only the driver was admitted to heaven. The reason? He had led far more people to pray.

Six kilometres from Port de Pollença you reach the Mirador des Colomer – scramble up the steps for views over a rocky islet. A path opposite the steps leads to an old watchtower from which you can see the whole of the peninsula as well as the bays of Pollença and Alcúdia. The road continues through pine woods and past more *miradors* (each one helpfully indicated with a picture of an old-fashioned camera) before tunnelling through En Fumat mountain, where you look down over Mallorca's most inaccessible beach. Eventually you reach a lighthouse with the inevitable bar and shop and more stunning views, all the way to Menorca on a good day.

On the way back, stop at Formentor beach and the Hotel Formentor, which opened in 1929 and has been pampering the rich and famous ever since. The fine sandy beach used to be reserved for the hotel's guests, but democracy has opened it to the masses.

4
Castell d'Alaró

A popular walk to a ruined castle and hilltop chapel offering spectacular views all the way to the sea.

A castle has stood on this site since Moorish times; it was so impregnable that the Arab commander was able to hold out for two years after the Christian conquest. Later, in 1285, two heroes of Mallorcan independence, Cabrit and Brassa, defended the castle against Alfonsó III of Aragón and were burned alive on a spit when he finally took it by storm. Their punishment was a consequence of their impudent defiance of the king. They pretended to confuse Alfonso's name with that of a local fish – *anfós*, shouting: 'We like our *anfós* grilled.' The present ruins date from the 15th century and seem almost to grow out of the rock, dominating the landscape for miles around.

The climb up here is one of Mallorca's most popular walks, especially on Sundays. From the town of Alaró it is a stiff climb of about two hours, following the signs from the PM210 to Orient; you can also leave from Orient (▶ 63), following a small path opposite L'Hermitage hotel, again taking around two hours in total. The paths converge above Es Verger restaurant (you can even bring a car this far if you don't mind the potholes and the hairpin bends), where you can fill up with roast lamb to fortify you for the final steep climb.

At last you reach the castle, 800m above sea level; look back at the view, stretching across the entire plain to Palma and out to sea. A few minutes further brings you to the summit, with a small chapel and sanctuary, and (bliss!) a restaurant and bar. If you are inspired by the views, you can stay the night here in one of the simple rooms.

✚ 28C4

☎ Sanctuary: 971 182112

🕐 Open access

🍴 Es Verger (€€)) on the way up; simple restaurant (€€) at the sanctuary

🚌 From Palma to Alaró

↔ Orient (▶ 63)

The final steps of the climb – almost time for a well-earned drink at the hilltop bar

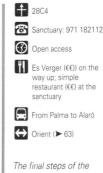

5
Castell de Bellver

➕ 28B3

✉ Parc Bellver

☎ 971 730657

🕐 Apr–Sep, Mon–Sat 8–8:30; Oct–Mar, Mon–Sat 8–7:15

🚌 3 or 6 to Plaça Gomila, or city sightseeing bus direct to the castle

🚾 Cheap. Free entrance on Sun, when museum closed

❓ Evening concerts in Jul, Aug

A well-preserved 14th-century royal fortress with fragrant pine woods, an interesting museum and superb views over Palma Bay.

Looking up at this castle, so perfectly maintained, it is hard to believe that it has been standing for almost 700 years. Begun by Jaume II in 1300 and built by Pere Salvà, the architect of the Almudaina Palace, it is unique among Spanish castles in being entirely round. Three large towers surround a central courtyard, connected by an arch to a free-standing keep. The courtyard itself is on two levels, the ground floor with semicircular arches and a flat roof, the upper level with Gothic arches and rib vaulting. For the full effect, walk around the moat then climb onto the roof and look down into the courtyard to compare the contrasting styles. While you are there, look out over the city and the bay for one of the best views in Palma (Bellver means 'lovely view' in Catalan).

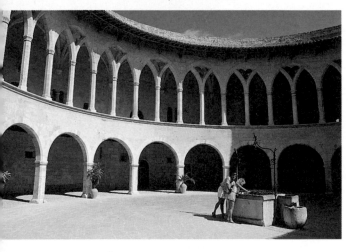

Bellver Castle has been both a royal residence and a military prison, but its main function now is as a historical museum

For many centuries the castle was used as a prison; Jaume III's widow and sons were imprisoned here for most of their lives. These days it contains Palma's museum of municipal history which traces the development of the city through its artefacts, with pottery from Talaiotic, Roman, Arab and Spanish periods.

You can get there by car or taxi, or take a bus to Plaça Gomila and climb up through the pine woods above Carrer de Bellver, passing a chapel on the way.

6
Coves d'Artà

A fascinating network of underground caverns, whose weird stalactites and stalagmites conjure up mysterious images of Heaven and Hell.

If you only have time to visit one set of caves on the east coast, this is the one to see. Now that they are a sanitised tourist attraction, it is hard to imagine how French geologist Édouard Martel felt when he first stepped into these caves, dark, mysterious and terrifying, in 1876. In fact they had been known about for centuries – Jaume I found 2,000 Arabs hiding here with their cattle during the Christian conquest and they were later used by hermits, pirates and smugglers – but it was Martel who first studied and chronicled these grottoes, 46m above the sea at Cap Vermell, at the instigation of Archduke Ludwig Salvator. Another early visitor was Jules Verne; the caves are said to have inspired his *Journey to the Centre of the Earth*.

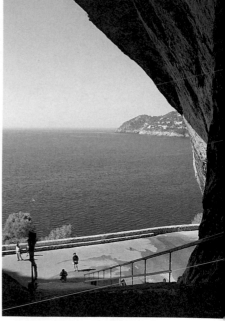

Back into daylight as you emerge from the caves

The guided tour comes with special effects and the various chambers are given Dantesque names – Hell, Purgatory, Paradise. The descent into Hell is swiftly followed by a *son et lumière* display. Stalactites point down from the mouldy roof like daggers, somehow defying gravity. One of the chambers is as large as the nave of Palma Cathedral, and the Queen of Pillars, a stalagmite 22m tall, could almost be a Gothic column. It is growing upwards at the rate of 2cm every 100 years; in another 5,000 years or so it will be joined to the ceiling.

You emerge from the caves to a view of the sea, framed by the cavern entrance. Disabled visitors and others with limited mobility will find the staircases in here particularly difficult. All visitors should be sensibly shod, as the floor can be slippery.

✚ 29F4

☎ 971 841293

🕐 Jul–Sep, daily 10–7; Oct–Jun, daily 10–5

🍴 Bars at Platja de Canyamel near by (€)

🚌 From Artà and Cala Rajada in summer

♿ None

✋ Expensive

7
Deià

*An idyllic village of green-shuttered,
ochre-coloured houses has become a millionaires'
hideaway in the shadow of the Teix mountain.*

 28B4

 Wide choice of
restaurants and bars
(€–€€€)

From Palma,
Valldemossa and Port
de Sóller

Lluc-Alcari (➤ 58), Son
Marroig (➤ 88)

Classical music festival
Aug–Sep

*Deià is a lot more
cosmopolitan than it looks*

Deià could have been just another pretty Mallorcan village
had Robert Graves not decided to make it his home. The
English poet and novelist first moved here in 1932 with his
mistress Laura Riding and returned in 1946 with his
second wife. Muses followed, friends came to stay, and
before long Deià had established a reputation as a foreign
artists' colony. Now it is on every tourist itinerary as the
prime example of 'the other Mallorca' and this small village
contains two luxury hotels. Rich foreign residents, like the
actor Michael Douglas, are apt to bemoan the arrival of
tour buses; the few locals who remain are philosophical
about outsiders.

Graves was hardly the first to discover Deià. An 1878
guidebook noted its 'collection of strange and eccentric
foreigners' and it has stayed that way ever since. Climb
the Carrer es Puig, Deià's only real street, passing ceramic
Stations of the Cross, to reach the parish church and the
small cemetery where Graves is buried. His tombstone,
like many others, is inscribed in simple handwriting set into
the drying concrete – *Robert Graves, Poeta, 1895–1985*.
Graves' house, Ca n'Alluny, has been acquired by the
government and is due to open as a museum in 2005.

From Deià you can scramble down to Cala de Deià, a
small shingle beach set in an attractive cove, where local
artists still continue the Graves tradition of naked
swimming and long parties at weekends.

8
Lluc

Mallorca's most sacred site –
a former monastery in a spectacular setting in the
Serra de Tramuntana.

Lluc has been a centre of pilgrimage since the 13th century when an Arab shepherd boy, newly converted to Christianity, discovered a dark wooden statue of the Virgin in a cleft in the rock. The image was placed in the local church but three times it returned miraculously to its cave, whereupon the villagers recognised a message from God and built a chapel to house it.

La Moreneta ('the Little Dark One') is now encrusted with precious stones, and sits in a chapel decorated with the arms of every Mallorcan town. Pilgrims and tourists queue to pay homage, especially on Sundays and at 11AM before the daily concerts by Els Blauets choir. The choir, named after their blue cassocks, was established in 1531, comprising 40 boys, 'natives of Mallorca, of pure blood, sound in grammar and song'. The service is marred by the whirring and flashing of cameras, and if it's meditation you seek, come back instead for the evening Mass.

The monastery complex includes Els Porxets, the former pilgrims' quarters with stabling beneath the rooms, and the Way of the Rosary, with touches by Antoni Gaudí. From the hilltop cross you look down over an unexpected farmland valley and up into the pine-covered mountains. You can stay at Lluc but it is more like a hotel than a hermitage – the 100 'cells' have *en suite* bathrooms and there are several restaurants and bars. There is also a **museum** – among the displays of ceramics, chalices and coins is a collection of paintings by the 20th-century Mallorcan artist Josep Coll Bardolet, with scenes from Deià, Valldemossa and Fornalutx.

The chapel at Lluc is
dedicated to the Virgin Mary

➕ 28C5

☎ 971 871525

🕐 Museum: daily 10–1:30, 2:30–5:15. Monastery: daily 9–8:30

🍴 Sa Fonda (€€) in the former monks' refectory

🚌 Two buses daily from Palma and Inca

✋ Monastery: free; Museum: cheap

❓ Choir concert daily 11:15 followed by Mass at 11:30; second service at dusk open to those staying; annual night-time pilgrimage from Palma to Lluc on foot (48km) – usually held in first week of Aug

9
La Seu (Palma Cathedral)

> *The glory of Palma – a magnificent Gothic
> cathedral whose sandstone walls and flying
> buttresses seem to rise out of the sea.*

Anything you see inside Palma cathedral will come as a
disappointment once you have stood on the seafront and
gazed up at its golden sandstone exterior, climbing above
the old city walls. La Seu stands out utterly from its
surroundings, a demonstration of the might of Mallorca's
Christian conquerors to all who arrived by sea.

Tradition has it that a storm arose as Jaume I was
sailing towards Mallorca. He vowed that if he landed safely
he would build a great church in honour of the Virgin. On
New Year's Day 1230, a day after the fall of Palma, the
foundation stone was symbolically laid on the site of the

city's main mosque. Work continued for 400 years – and had to resume in 1851 when an earthquake destroyed the west front. More touches were added in the 20th century by the Catalan architect Antoni Gaudí.

You enter through a side door, passing a small museum; head for the west portal and gaze down the long nave. Light pours in through the rose window, one of the world's largest, 12m across and studded with 1,236 pieces of stained glass. The columns are ringed with wrought-iron candelabra by Gaudí; his most controversial addition is the unfinished Crown of Thorns, fashioned from cardboard and cork and suspended above the altar.

Be sure to walk around to the south front, facing the sea, to look at the Portal del Mirador, a 15th-century door by Guillem Sagrera featuring scenes from the Last Supper.

34B2

Plaça d'Almoina

971 723130

Jun–Sep, Mon–Fri 10–6:15, Sat 10–2:15; Apr–May and Oct, Mon–Fri 10–5:15, Sat 10–2:15; Nov–Mar, Mon–Fri 10–3:15, Sat 10–2:15

Few

Moderate (free for services)

Museu Diocesà (➤ 37), Palau de l'Almudaina (➤ 38), Palau March (➤ 38)

High Mass, Sun 10:30

Even the royal palace is cut down to size by the mystery of Palma cathedral, standing out above its surroundings on the waterfront

25

10
Valldemossa

 28B4

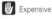

🍴 Choice of restaurants and bars (€€)

🚌 From Palma, Deià and Port de Sóller

❓ Regular Chopin piano concerts in Palau del Rei Sanç (entered on same ticket as monastery); La Beata procession in honour of Santa Catalina Thomás, 27–28 Jul; Chopin Festival in Aug; market held Sun

Reial Cartoixa

☎ 971 612106

🕐 Mar–Oct, Mon–Sat 9:30–6, Sun 10–1; Nov–Feb, Mon–Sat 9:30–4:30

✋ Expensive

The small town in the mountains where Mallorcan tourism began one cold, damp winter in 1838.

Try as it might – and it doesn't try very hard – Valldemossa cannot escape its connection with Frédéric Chopin and his lover George Sand. They arrived in 1838, having rented a former monk's cell, planning to carry on their affair away from the gossip of Paris and hoping that the climate would benefit Chopin's health (he had tuberculosis). Nothing worked out as planned. The weather was wet and windy, the couple were shunned by the locals, Chopin's piano failed to arrive and the relationship never recovered. Sand took out her anger on Valldemossa in a spiteful book, *Winter in Majorca*, which the locals, labelled as thieves and savages, still gleefully sell to visitors.

The **Reial Cartoixa** (Royal Carthusian Monastery) is the focus of any visit – white-arched corridors lead to 'cells' containing museums on various themes. Visit the old pharmacy – you can almost smell the herbs – then look into the library, where the monks would meet for half an hour a week, their only human contact. There is a fine modern art museum, with works by Picasso, Miró and Juli Ramis, and of course there is Chopin's cell...

Most people come for the Chopin experience, but there is more to Valldemossa than that. It is also the birthplace of Catalina Thomás, Mallorca's patron saint. A peasant girl born in 1531, she became a nun in Palma and was renowned for her humility. Almost every home in Valldemossa has a plaque imploring her prayers, and her birthplace at Carrer Rectoría 5 has been turned into a shrine. She would probably be appalled.

The newest attraction in Valldemossa is Michael Douglas' Costa Nord (▶ 51).

The Carthusian monastery stands at the centre of the highest town in Mallorca

What To See

Above: *Hairpin bends on the way down to Sa Calobra;*
Right: *Monument, Santa Ponça*

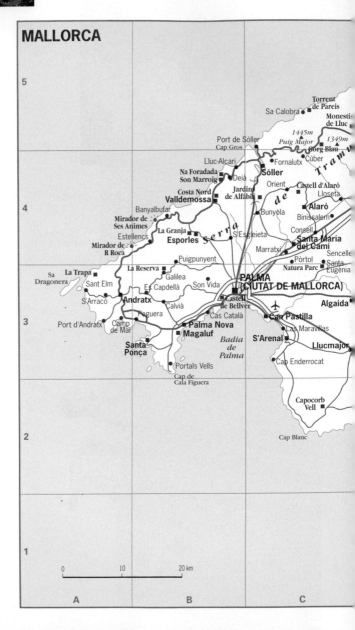

MALLORCA

5

Torrent
de Pareis
Sa Calobra
Monesti
de Lluc

1445m *1349m*
Puig Major Gorg Blau
Port de Sóller
Cap Gros

Lluc-Alcari Cúber
Fornalutx
Na Foradada Sóller
Son Marroig Deià
Costa Nord Jardins Orient Castell d'Alaró
Valldemossa de Alfàbia Lloseta

Banyalbufar Alaró
Mirador de Bunyola Binissalem
Ses Animes
Estellencs La Granja S'Esgleieta Consell Santa María
Esporles del Camí
Mirador de Marratxí Sencelle
R Roca Puigpunyent Pòrtol Santa
La Reserva Natura Parc Eugènia
Sa La Trapa Galilea
Dragonera Sant Elm Son Vida PALMA
Es Capdellà (CIUTAT DE MALLORCA)
S'Arracó Castell Algaida
Andratx de Bellver
Calvià Cás Català Can Pastilla
Port d'Andratx Peguera
Camp Palma Nova Las Maravillas
de Mar Magaluf S'Arenal Llucmajor
Santa Badia
Ponça de Cap Enderrocat
Portals Vells Palma
Cap de
Cala Figuera

4

3

Capocorb
Vell

2

Cap Blanc

1

0   10   20 km

A   B   C

Cap de Formentor
Mirador des Colomer
Cala de Sant Vicenç
Formentor
Castell del Rei
Port de Pollença
Pollença
Puig de Maria
Badia de Pollença
Cap des Pinar
Ermita de la Victoria
Alcúdia
Port d'Alcúdia
Coves de Campanet
Badia d'Alcúdia
Cap de Ferrutx
S'ALBUFERA
Platja de Murro
Can Picafort
Selva
Sa Pobla
Ermita de Betlem
Cap des Freu
Muro
Colònia de Sant Pere
Cala Rajada
Ermita de Santa Magdalena
Inca
Santa Margalida
Artà
Capdepera
Punta de Capdepera
Llubí
Ses Païsses
Coves d'Artà
Cap Vermell
María de la Salut
Son Servera
Sa Costa des Pins
Sineu
Cala Bona
Petra
Sant Llorenç des Cardassar
Auto-Safari
Cala Millor
Pina
Sant Joan
Ermita de Bonany
Sa Coma
Punta de n'Amer
Montuïri
Vilafranca de Bonany
Manacor
Coves dels Hams
Santuari de Cura
543m
Puig de Randa
Porreres
Porto Cristo
Coves del Drac
Randa
509m
Puig de Sant Salvador
Felanitx
Santuari de Sant Salvador
Porto Colom
Campos
Castell de Santueri
Vernissa
Cala d'Or
Sa Ràpita
Ses Covetes
Porto Petro
Platja des Trenc
Ses Salines
Santanyí
Cala Mondragó
Colònia de Sant Jordi
Botanicáctus
Cala Figuera
Cala Santanyí
Cala Llombards
Cap de Ses Salines

Freu de Cabrera
Sa Conillera
Cabrera

D   E   F

29

Palma

Palma comes as a surprise to many people – it is stylish, sophisticated, intimate yet bursting with life. Half of Mallorca's population live here, enjoying the island's best restaurants, shops and nightlife as well as a thriving arts scene and a lively café society.

Palma's masterpiece is its Gothic cathedral, rising out of the city walls which once marked the edge of the sea. Close to here is the old Arab quarter, its maze of narrow streets hiding museums, palaces and exquisite courtyards. But do not explore old Palma at the expense of its modern side. Take coffee in the former Gran Hotel, visit an art gallery in a converted mansion, join Palma's bright young things on their evening *passeig* along the waterfront, and you will begin to appreciate the variety of this fascinating city.

> *'The time will doubtless come when frail dilettantes, and even lovely women, will be able to visit Palma with no more exhaustion and discomfort than Geneva.'*
>
> GEORGE SAND
> *Winter in Majorca* (1855), translated
> by Robert Graves (1956)

Palma

Known to the Arabs as Medina Mayurqa and to Mallorcans simply as *Ciutat* (City), Palma is in fact named after the Roman city of Palmaria. Here you can almost literally uncover the different layers of Mallorcan history. The Roman city still exists, a metre or two beneath the ground; inhabitants of houses near the cathedral are still discovering Roman remains. The cathedral was built on the site of a mosque, once a Roman temple; the royal palace replaced an Arab *alcázar*.

The city you see today, however, is a relatively recent creation. The tree-lined promenades of La Rambla and Passeig des Born, home to florists and newspaper sellers, were built in the 19th century on a dried-up river bed. The walls which once surrounded the city were pulled down to create the ring road Las Avingudas, and Passeig Marítim, the waterfront highway and promenade, was only reclaimed from the sea in the 1950s.

Most of the main sights are located within the area bounded by the old walls, especially to the north and east of the cathedral. Wander along any alley in the ancient Arab quarter, peering through wrought-iron gates and heavy wooden doors, and you will be rewarded with glimpses of one magnificent patio after another, with their stone staircases, galleries and arcades.

But you have not truly seen Palma until you have surveyed it from the waterfront, with the cathedral and Almudaina palace rising proudly above the defensive walls of the old city, their golden sandstone lit up by the afternoon sun.

Palma's pedestrian shopping streets seem designed for browsing – but everything stops during the afternoon siesta

What to See in Palma

BANYS ÀRABS (ARAB BATHS) ✪✪

These 10th-century baths are virtually all that remain of the Arab city of Medina Mayurqa. They were probably part of a nobleman's house and are similar to those found in other Islamic cities. The *tepidarium* has a dome in the shape of a half-orange, with 25 round shafts for sunlight, supported by a dozen columns. Notice how each of the columns is different – they were probably salvaged from the ruins of various Roman buildings, an early example of recycling. *Hammams* were meeting places as well as wash-houses, and the courtyard with its cactus, palm and orange trees would have made a pleasant place to cool off after a hot bath.

BASÍLICA DE SANT FRANCESC ✪✪

The façade of this 13th-century church (remodelled after it was struck by lightning in the 17th century) is typically Mallorcan – a massive, forbidding sandstone wall with a delicately carved portal and a rose window at the centre. You enter through peaceful Gothic cloisters with orange and lemon trees and a well at the centre. Inside the church

is the tomb of Ramón Llull (1235–1316), the Catalan mystic who became a hermit following a failed seduction attempt and was later stoned to death attempting to convert Muslims in Tunisia. His statue can be seen on the Palma seafront; outside the basilica is a statue of another famous Mallorcan missionary, Fray Junípero Serra, who once lived in the monastery here. The streets behind the church, once home to jewellers and Jewish traders, are now rundown and seedy and best avoided after dark.

CASTELL DE BELLVER
(► 20, TOP TEN)

An impressive baroque portal gives relief to the stern façade of Palma's mighty Basílica de Sant Francesc

---

Banys Àrabs

+ 35C1
✉ Carrer Can Serra 7
☎ 971 721549
🕐 Daily 9–8
🍴 Bar Sa Murada near by (€)
♿ None
💷 Cheap
↔ Museu de Mallorca (► 37)

Basílica de Sant Francesc

+ 35C2
✉ Plaça Sant Francesc
☎ 971 712695
🕐 Mon–Sat 9:30–12:30, 3:30–6, Sun 9:30–12:30
💷 Cheap

ES BALUARD ✪✪✪

Opened in 2004 and set inside the restored 16th-century bastion of Sant Pere, this museum dramatically combines military architecture with modern art. The displays vary but will probably include work by Picasso, Joan Miró and Miquel Barceló. A walk around the walls offers spectacular views over the bay, and there are more good views from the sculpture terrace.

➕ 34A3
✉ Plaça Porta de Santa Catalina
☎ 971 908200
🕐 Jun–Sep, 10–midnight; Oct–May, Tue–Sun 10–8
♿ Good ✋ Moderate

FUNDACIÓ LA CAIXA ✪✪✪

The Gran Hotel was Palma's first luxury hotel when it opened in 1903. Designed by the Catalan architect Lluís Domènech i Montaner, it began the craze for *modernista* (art nouveau) architecture in the city. Restored by the Fundació la Caixa and reopened in 1993, it is now an art gallery with changing exhibitions and paintings by Hermen Anglada-Camarasa, founder of the 'Pollença school'. On the ground floor there is a bookshop and a trendy café-bar.

➕ 35C3
✉ Plaça Weyler 3
☎ 971 178500
🕐 Tue–Sat 10–9, Sun 10–2
🍴 Café and restaurant (€€)
♿ Good
✋ Free

LA LLOTJA ✪✪

With twin turrets and an angel over the door, this 15th-century seafront building looks half-castle, half-church. In fact it is neither. It was designed by Guillem Sagrera (the architect of the cathedral's Portal del Mirador) as the city's exchange. Stand among the spiralling pillars, gaze up at the rib vaulting, and try to imagine the merchants of 500 years ago haggling over silk, spices and silver. Nowadays La Llotja is a cultural centre, hosting temporary exhibitions.

➕ 34A2
✉ Plaça Llotja
🕐 Hours vary according to exhibition
🍴 Wide choice of restaurants and bars near by (€–€€)
♿ Good
✋ Free

Modern art, inside and out, at Fundació la Caixa – the 'in' place to meet for coffee and cakes

Canòdrom

Institut Provincial Ramón Llull

VIA PORTUGAL

San Sebastián

PLAÇA FORTI

C. BISBE CAMPINS

Jardí Botànic

Policía Nacional

RUIZ DE ALDA

Hospital Provincial

La Concepció

AVINGUDA JAUME III

Sant Jaume

PLAÇA REI JOAN CARLES I

San Cayetano

Santa Cruz

Ca'n Solleric

Sant Nicolau

Baluard Sant Pere

Consulat del Mar

PLAÇA DE LA REINA

CONQUISTADOR

La Llotja

PLAÇA LLOTJA

Llotja del Pescado

Palau de l'Almudaina

La Seu (Catedral)

PASSEIG URUGUAY

PALMA CITY CENTRE

0   200   400 m

A   B

A statue of a Roman emperor stands at the foot of La Rambla

**Map labels:**

ALEMANYA
COMTE DE SALLENT
BLANQUERNA
31 DE DICIEMBRE
JARDI DE LLUIS SALVADOR
AV JUAN MARCH
EUSEBIO ESTADA
Estació de Autobúses
PLAÇA CONQUISTA
Parc de les Estacions
Hospital Militar
SANT MIQUEL
PLAÇA D'ESPANYA
Santa Catalina
AVINGUDA ALEXANDRE
ROSSELLÓ
Santa Magdalena
RAMBLA
PLAÇA DEL OLIVAR
Col·lecció March
Parc de la Mar
Sant Miquel
SINDICAT
Fundació Joan March
La Mercet
Fundació la Caixa / Gran Hotel
Teatre Principal
UNIÓ
PLAÇA WEYLER
PLAÇA MAJOR
PLAÇA DE SANT ANTONIO
PLAÇA DEL MERCAT
Palau de Justicia
Santa Eulàlia
Palau Vivot
PLAÇA QUADRADO
VILLALONGA
i PLAÇA CORT
Ajuntament
PLAÇA SANTA EULÀLIA
PLAÇA SANT FRANCESC
Basílica de Sant Francesc
Socorro
ALOMAR
Arc de l'Almudaina
Museu Diocesà
Museu de Mallorca
El Temple
Montesió
Banys Àrabs
Santa Clara
San Jerónimo
AVINGUDA DE GABRIEL
JOAN MARAGALL
Parc de la Mar

C   D

A Walk Around Palma

Distance
3.5km

Time
2 hours plus coffees,
browsing and visits – probably
half a day

Start/end point
Plaça d'Espanya
 35D4
Most city buses
terminate here; island
buses terminate at the
nearby bus station on
Carrer Eusebi Estada
Trains from Inca and
Sóller also terminate here

Lunch
Fundació la Caixa (€)
Plaça Weyler 3
971 728077

Start om Plaça d'Espanya by the statue of Jaume I the Conqueror on horseback. With the station behind you, bear left across the square towards Mercat Olivar (▶ 37).

Leave via Plaça Olivar and turn left into Carrer Sant Miquel.

Soon you reach Plaça Major with its outdoor cafés and street entertainers.

Continue across the square; fork right into Carrer Jaume II.

At the end of this pedestrian shopping street, don't fail to look up at the Moorish-style *modernista* façade of Can Corbella before turning left into Plaça Cort. Beyond a gnarled olive tree you see the town hall.

Take the short street to the left of the town hall to reach Plaça Santa Eulàlia; cross this square diagonally and take Carrer Morey.

This brings you into the heart of the old city. Take your time here admiring the courtyards; don't miss Casa Oleza at No. 9.

Continue straight on to Carrer Miramar and turn right onto the city walls.

The cathedral (▶ 24–25) is above you; to visit it and the palace, climb the steps to a large wooden cross.

Plaça Major – a good place to stop for a coffee. There is a craft market held here on summer mornings

Back on the walls, continue until you drop to the S'Hort del Rei gardens (▶ 38). Cross Plaça Reina and walk up the Born (▶ 39), turning right by Bar Bosch into Carrer Unió.

Look out for the old Gran Hotel (▶ 33) on your left and the bakery opposite, two good examples of *modernista* style. Beyond the theatre, the road bends left and becomes La Rambla; stroll up this promenade among the flower stalls.

At the top of La Rambla, turn right into Carrer Oms and follow it back to Plaça d'Espanya.

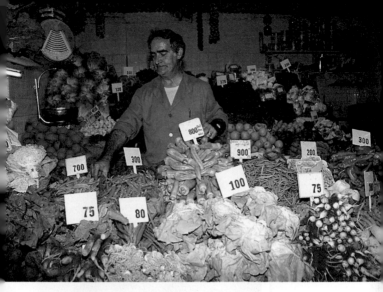

Fresh vegetables on sale in Mercat Olivar

MERCAT OLIVAR ✪✪

When you're tired of museums and churches and want to meet the people of Palma instead, head for this large covered market near Plaça d'Espanya. After a recent renovation, there is now a supermarket on the first floor and the ground-floor stalls have been spruced up but the market has lost none of its atmosphere. Huge piles of oranges and tomatoes, buckets full of olives, meat and cheese counters and fresh fish stalls in a separate annex all add up to a visual feast. There are also several traditional *tapas* bars, where the market workers can still be seen drinking brandy with their breakfast coffee

✚ 35D4
✉ Plaça Olivar
☎ 971 720315
🕐 Mon–Sat 8–2
🍴 Several *tapas* bars (€) upstairs
🖐 Free

MUSEU D'ART ESPANYOL CONTEMPORANI ✪✪

The private collection of Mallorcan banker Joan March (1880-1962) has been expanded into this small museum of 20th-century Spanish art close to Plaça Major. Among the artists represented are Picasso, Joan Miró and Salvador Dalí, Catalan abstract artist Antoni Tàpies and Basque sculptor Eduardo Chillida. A room is dedicated to Miquel Barceló, the avant-garde painter born in Mallorca in 1957.

✚ 35C3
✉ Carror Sant Miquel 11
☎ 971 713515
🕐 Mon–Fri 10–6.30, Sat 10.30–2
🖐 Free

MUSEU DE MALLORCA ✪✪✪

Mallorca's most important museum is housed in a 17th-century palace, with collections spanning more than 3,000 years of history. Start in the basement with the prehistory section, which includes pottery, metal and stone artefacts from the Talaiotic cultures, as well as bronze figures of naked warriors brought back from the Punic wars. Other rooms are devoted to Islamic archaeology, Gothic art (with a particularly fine collection of painted altarpieces), Modernism and 20th-century art.

✚ 35C2
✉ Carrer Portella 5
☎ 971 717540
🕐 Tue–Sat 10–7, Sun 10–2
🍴 Bar Sa Murada (€) at foot of Carrer Portella
🖐 Cheap

37

Palma's royal palace was built as a Muslim fortress and still has a very Islamic feel to it

 34B2
⊠ Carrer Palau Reial
☎ 971 214134
🕐 Palace: Apr–Oct, Mon–Fri 10–6:30, Sat 10–2; Nov–Mar, Mon–Fri 10–2, 4–6, Sat 10–2; Gardens: open access
♿ Wheelchair access on request
💷 Palace: moderate; Gardens: free
↔ La Seu (► 24–25), Palau March (► below)
❓ Still used by King Juan Carlos for official functions in Palma

PALAU DE L'ALMUDAINA

A royal palace has stood on this site since the Muslim *walis* (governors) built their *alcázar* soon after the Arab conquest. It was converted into Gothic style under Jaume II, but elements of Islamic architecture remain – like the Moorish arches seen from the seafront, lit up at night like a row of lanterns. The courtyard, laid out in 1309 and flanked by palm trees, is at its best in late afternoon when the sun falls on the cathedral towers overhead. Just off the courtyard is the royal chapel, Capella de Santa Ana.

The S'Hort del Rei gardens beneath the palace make a pleasant place to sit beneath the fountains watching the world go by. Look out for the Arc de la Drassana, once the gateway to the royal docks; near here is a statue of a *hondero* or Balearic slinger. The gardens were rebuilt in the 1960s, forcing the demolition of several houses; their best-known landmark is Joan Miró's *Egg* sculpture, which few people can resist sticking their heads through.

🔲 35B2
⊠ Carrer Palau Reial 18
☎ 971 711122
🕐 Mon–Fri 10–6, Sat 10–2
🍴 Cappuccino Palau March (€)
💷 Moderate
↔ La Seu (► 24–25), Palau de L'Almudaina (► above)

PALAU MARCH

This quirky and enjoyable museum reflects the eclectic tastes of the banker Joan March and his son Bartolomé. Most striking is the sculpture terrace, in an open courtyard surrounded by an attractive loggia in the shadow of the cathedral. Among the artists represented are Rodin, Henry Moore, Barbara Hepworth and contemporary Spanish sculptors. Highlights include the collection of miniature Neapolitan crib figures, 16th-century Mallorcan maps, and the original 1940s murals for the Music Room by Josep Maria Sert, with their acrobats and carnival scenes.

PASSEIG DES BORN ⚫⚫

For more than a century this short, tree-lined promenade has been at the heart of city life; it has witnessed *festas*, demonstrations and countless generations of families enjoying an evening stroll. During the Franco era it was renamed after the dictator, but everyone still called it 'the Born'. Come here to take the pulse of Palma from a seat at a pavement café – Bar Bosch, near the top of the Born in Plaça Rei Joan Carles I, is the traditional place. Near here is **Ca'n Solleric**, a modern art gallery in a converted mansion that also houses the city's tourist office.

➕ 34B3
🍴 Wide choice of restaurants and cafés near by (€–€€)

Ca'n Solleric
✉ Passeig des Born 27
☎ 971 722092
🕐 Tue–Sat 10–2, 5–9, Sun 10–1:30
🎟 Free

POBLE ESPANYOL (SPANISH VILLAGE) ⚫

Spain gets the theme-park treatment at this 'village' in the outskirts of Palma, where reproductions of famous buildings from Córdoba, Toledo and Madrid are gathered together with typical houses from the Spanish regions. You can eat Spanish food in the Plaza Mayor (Spanish spellings here) or sit outside a café watching the tourists buy pearls and souvenirs at the village shops. A visit here gives you a whistle-stop tour of Spanish architecture, showing its development through Muslim and then Christian influences. If you have never been to Granada, it's worth coming just for the reproduction of the salon, baths and patio from the Alhambra Palace. Various artists give displays of handicrafts in workshops scattered throughout the 'village'.

➕ 72B2
✉ Carrer Poble Espanyol
☎ 971 737075
🕐 Apr–Nov, daily 9–7; Dec–Mar, daily 9–6
🍴 Restaurant and cafés (€€)
🔢 5
🎟 Moderate
❓ Craft displays from 10 to one hour before closing time

LA SEU (► 24–25, TOP TEN)

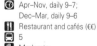

'The Born' once hosted jousting contests but now the biggest battle is for a seat at a pavement café

A Walk by the Sea

Distance
3km one way

Time
1½ hours

Start point
Parc de la Mar
✚ 34B1

End point
Club de Mar
🚌 1

Lunch
Taberna de la Boveda (€€)
✉ Passeig Sagrera 3
☎ 971 720026

This walk along Palma's waterfront is good in the early morning, as the city stirs itself and the fish market comes to life; or late in the day as the sun sets over the sea, the pavement bars begin to buzz and the cathedral and castle light up for the night.

Start on Parc de la Mar, gazing across at the cathedral reflected in an artificial lake. Cross Avinguda d'Antoni Maura to reach Passeig Sagrera.

This short tree-lined avenue, named after the architect of La Llotja, passes several interesting buildings. First, La Llotja itself (▶ 33), Palma's masterpiece of Gothic civic architecture; Porta Vella del Moll, the old gateway to the city from the sea; and finally Consulat del Mar, the former maritime court which houses the Balearic government.

At the end of Passeig Sagrera, cross the main road to reach the fishing port, marked by lines of blue nets.

West of here, in a small garden, is the oratory of Sant Elm, designed as a navigators' chapel, later used as a tavern, and moved here stone by stone.

From here the walk is straightforward – just follow the seafront west along Passeig Marítim, using the promenade between the road and the sea. A cycle path, also used by joggers, runs alongside the promenade.

Pass Reial Club Nautic, facing a section of city wall and a row of windmills; look up ahead to see Bellver Castle on its hill. As you walk on, turn around to look back at the cathedral, seen across the bay through a forest of masts. From a jetty opposite the Auditorium theatre, excursion boats offer tours of Palma Bay. Keep going, and eventually you reach the marina with its luxury yachts. Just beyond here is the commercial ferry port, where boats leave for Barcelona, Valencia, Menorca and Ibiza.

Return the same way, or take bus 1 back to Passeig Sagrera.

Around the Island

Each region of Mallorca has its own particular appeal – the northeast for history, the east coast for beaches and caves, the north and west for spectacular mountains and picture-postcard villages. And you haven't seen Mallorca until you have driven across *es pla*, the fertile plain at the centre of the island, with its almond groves, windmills and old market towns.

Try to do a bit of everything – one monastery, one mountain walk, one quiet cove – but don't try to do too much. The twisting mountain roads get very crowded in summer and journeys take longer than you think. Take your time and avoid the worst of the heat by doing what the Mallorcans do, break for a siesta. It is generally far more rewarding to spend a day pottering around one small area than to hare from one town to another ticking off the sights.

' If you would experience the most perfect method of travelling, ride upon a mule, under a Mediterranean sun, along a golden road that leads down from the mountains to the sea. '

GORDON WEST
Jogging Round Majorca (1929)

What to See Around the Island

ALCÚDIA (► 16, TOP TEN)

ALGAIDA ✪

Algaida is a typical Mallorcan town, all green shutters, narrow streets, a square lined with cafés and a huge sandstone church. Few visitors make it into the town centre; the attractions are all on the outskirts, on the Palma–Manacor road. The main one is Ca'n Gordiola, a glass factory housed in a mock castle. The ground floor contains a workshop (though it looks more like a church with its arches and stained glass) where you can watch glass being blown; upstairs there is a museum devoted to the history of glass making around the world. A further 2km along the road to Manacor is a string of well-known restaurants, where the people of Palma head at weekends for old-fashioned Mallorcan cuisine.

ANDRATX ✪

Like many towns around the coast, Andratx was built several kilometres inland from its port in a bid to deter pirate raids. These days the town is reaping an unexpected benefit – tourists pour into the port, spending money which the town collects in taxes, yet except on market day Andratx sees little of the visitors and its people are left to get on with their lives. Surrounded by orange groves, and almond trees which leave a 'snowfall' of blossom each February, Andratx is a sleepy town which only really gets animated on Wednesdays when the streets are taken over by market stalls selling vegetables, cheeses and fish. When you have finished your shopping, climb to the top of the town to see the 13th-century church of Santa Maria.

✚ 28C3
🍴 Restaurants on the
   Palma–Manacor road (€)
🚌 From Palma
↔ Puig de Randa (► 75)
❓ Market held Fri

Ca'n Gordiola
✉ Carretera Palma–
   Manacor, km19
☎ 971 665046
🕐 Apr–Oct, Mon–Sat
   9–7:30, Sun 9–12;
   Nov–Mar, Mon–Sat
   9–1:30, 3–7, Sun 9–12
✋ Free

✚ 28A3
🍴 Bars and cafés (€)
🚌 Regular buses from
   Palma, Peguera and Port
   d'Andratx
↔ Port d'Andratx (► 67),
   Sant Elm (► 79)
❓ Market held Wed

*Almonds from the
orchards around Andratx
are one of the bargains
you can pick up in the
weekly market*

The West

Distance
62km

Time
3 hours plus lunch and time at La Granja

Start/end point
Andratx
✛ 28A3

Lunch
La Granja (€)
☎ 971 610032

You pass several coastal watchtowers, including this one near the village of Estellencs

This drive gives an excellent introduction to the mountain and coastal scenery of western Mallorca.

Start in Andratx, taking the C710 to Estellencs about halfway up the main street.

Immediately the road begins to climb through pine woods and tunnels, with occasional glimpses of the sea. Follow this beautiful twisting coast road to the village of Estellencs, one of the prettiest in Mallorca, with narrow, steep cobbled streets and women doing their washing at the village well. After another 5km, stop at the Mirador de Ses Animes and clamber up to the 16th-century watch-tower for views right along the northwest coast. Soon after this you reach Banyalbufar (► 46), with its spectacular terracing.

When the C710 turns off left towards Valldemossa, keep straight on the PM110, signposted to Palma. After 1km you see a sign to La Granja on your right.

You could easily spend 2–3 hours at this display of Mallorcan traditions (► 57).

Leaving La Granja, take the narrow road to Puigpunyent from the car park.

Follow this road for 10km, a dramatic journey through olive groves in the shadow of Puig de Galatzó. The road continues through Puigpunyent and on to Galilea (► 56), a mountain village with a couple of *tapas* bars and views out to sea. From here the road twists and turns down to the village of Es Capdella.

Turn right in the village and follow signs back to Andratx.

A flight of steps leads to Artà's hilltop sanctuary

ARTÀ ✪✪

Derived from the Arabic word *jertan* ('garden'), Artà has been occupied for at least 3,000 years, as evidenced by the remains of a Bronze Age site at Ses Païsses (▶ 85) just outside the town. Nowadays Artà is a prosperous little town near the coast, which gets particularly lively each Tuesday on market day.

From the parish church of Transfiguració del Senyor, an avenue of cypress trees leads to Artà's crowning glory, its hilltop fortress and Santuari de Sant Salvador. The view down over the rooftops, a jumble of tiles in every shade of brown, is one of the sights of Mallorca. On the site of a Moorish fortress, the original sanctuary walls and chapel were rebuilt in the 19th century. Walk around the battlements, rest in a peaceful courtyard, then look into the sanctuary church with its vivid paintings of two Mallorcan heroes – Jaume the Conqueror receiving the surrender of the *walis*, and Ramón Llull being stoned to death in Tunisia. There is also a painting of Sant Antoni, patron saint of Artà, and of animals, seen here, as always, with a small pig. Each January the saint is commemorated with a masked procession and a blessing of pets. Artà's big festival, Sant Antoni de Juny, dates back to 1581 and features dancers with cardboard horses strapped to their hips.

The coastline north of Artà contains some of Mallorca's wildest and most beautiful beaches, including the virgin cove of Cala Torta.

✚ 29E4
🍴 Several bars and restaurants (€–€€)
🚌 From Palma and Cala Rajada
↔ Ses Païsses (▶ 85)
❓ Market held Tue; Sant Antoni Abat, procession and blessing of pets, 16–17 Jan; Sant Antoni de Juny, *cavallets* horse dances, 13 Jun

AUTO-SAFARI (SAFARI-ZOO) ✪

Mallorca's only zoo consists of a 4-km drive through open countryside, passing giraffes, zebra, flamingos and deer (keep your car windows shut against marauding monkeys), followed by a 'baby zoo' with elephants, crocodiles and various young animals. You can also explore the 44-hectare reserve by a special 'mini-train' for which you pay a hefty supplement on top of the already considerable cost of entry.

✚ 29F3
✉ Carretera Porto Cristo–Son Servera, km5
☎ 971 810909
🕐 Apr–Sep, daily 9–7; Oct–Mar, daily 9–5
🍴 Café (€)
♿ Good
✋ Expensive

45

28B4
🍴 Café Bellavista (€)
🚌 Bus from Palma
↔ La Granja (▶ 57)

The terraced slopes of Banyalbufar, created over a thousand years, reach right down to the sea

➕ 28C4
🍴 Several restaurants and bars (€€)
🚂 Train from Palma and Inca
↔ Inca (▶ 58)
❓ Market held Fri; wine festival last weekend in Sep

➕ 29D1
🚢 From Colònia de Sant Jordi, May–Oct, daily 9:30 (☎ 971 649034)
↔ Colònia de Sant Jordi (▶ 51)

BANYALBUFAR ⊙⊙

People come to Banyalbufar to see one thing – its terraced hillsides, sloping down to the sea. Developed by the Moors and divided by drystone walls, these terraces speak powerfully of man's ingenuity in creating farmland out of inhospitable cliffs. Until recently it was the custom for each generation to add a further tier. In Moorish times the town, whose Arabic name means 'vineyard by the sea', was famed for its Malvasia wine – nowadays the terraces are mostly used to grow vegetables, though a few vines have been planted once again. Banyalbufar's popularity with foreign artists has led some people to conclude that it will be the next Deià (▶ 22).

BINISSALEM ⊙

If you order Mallorcan wine in a restaurant, it will probably come from Binissalem. Viticulture was introduced here by the Romans and has survived in much reduced form. The reputation of Binissalem red wines, made with the local grape Manto Negro, has been growing recently – the best-known *bodega*, José L Ferrer, offering tastings and guided tours, is on the right as you enter the town from Palma. Binissalem is a handsome town with a well-preserved old quarter in the streets around the church square.

CABRERA ⊙⊙

'Goat island' is the largest in a rocky archipelago lying 10km off the south coast. Pliny claimed it as the birthplace of Hannibal; during the Napoleonic Wars it became a notorious prison camp. Since 1991 the island has been a protected national park. You can only get there on a day trip by boat, with time to walk up to the 14th-century castle above the harbour, visit a museum housed in an old wine cellar and swim in the Blue Grotto on the way back.

CALA DE SANT VICENÇ ⊕⊕

This old-fashioned holiday resort has recently been given a facelift and is in danger of becoming chic. It is still very popular with Mallorcans, especially on summer weekends. Four small coves, each with their own beach, huddle together beneath Cavall Bernat, a limestone ridge which casts its shadow into the sea. A walk of around 45 minutes leads across the hills to Port de Pollença (► 70).

🔲 29D5
🍴 Bars and restaurants (€–€€€)
🚌 Bus from Pollença
🔄 Pollença (► 66), Port de Pollença (► 70)

CALA D'OR ⊕⊕

Each of the various *calas* (bays) along the east coast has its own distinctive character; in the case of Cala d'Or the word is 'chic'. Former fishing harbours have been turned into marinas; people come here to sail and dive, and drink champagne at waterfront bars. The villas are white and flat-roofed, in Ibizan style, designed in the 1930s by Pep Costa Ferrer, and the effect is surprisingly attractive. Nowadays Cala d'Or is the collective name for a string of resorts, beaches and coves; they include Porto Petro, around a horseshoe bay 2km to the south, and Cala Mondragó, a further 4km south, where a pair of sandy beaches form part of the Mondragó nature reserve.

🔲 29E2
🍴 Wide choice of restaurants (€€–€€€)
🚌 From Palma

CALA FIGUERA ⊕⊕

More than anywhere else in Mallorca, Cala Figuera retains the atmosphere of a working fishing port. White-painted houses reach down to the water's edge and fishermen sit on the steps mending nets. If you get here early enough in the morning you might even see the catch coming in. A path follows around the tiny harbour and onto the cliffs, offering good views back towards the bay. The nearest beach is 4km to the south at Cala Santanyí.

🔲 29E2
🍴 Several seafood restaurants and others (€€)
🚌 From Palma and Santanyí
🔄 Santanyí (► 82)

Fishermen's cottages at Cala Figuera

29F3

Wide choice of bars and
restaurants (€–€€)

From Palma; also from
Cala Rajada and Port
d'Alcúdia in summer

Punta de n'Amer (► 76)

*Cala Millor – the golden
sands just go on and on*

CALA MILLOR ✪

Fifty years ago this was a lonely dune-covered shore; now
it has become the major resort on Mallorca's east coast.
The main attraction is its fine sandy beaches; from Cala
Bona ('the good bay') to Cala Millor ('the better bay') they
stretch unbroken for 2km. In summer it is 'lively', travel-
agent speak for brash, and best avoided unless you like
discos and late-night bars; in winter it takes on a new
atmosphere, as a resort for the 'young at heart', another
travel-agent euphemism. To see what this coast used to
be like, walk to the headland at Punta de n'Amer (► 76).

29F4

Wide choice of
restaurants (€€)

From Palma and Porto
Cristo; also from Cala
Millor in summer

Day trips to Menorca
(☎ 902 100444)

Tourist office: Plaça dels
Pins (☎ 971 563033)

Capdepera (► 50)

Market held Sat; proces-
sions of boats, 16 July

CALA RAJADA ✪

This fishing port on Mallorca's eastern tip, surrounded by
fine beaches and pretty coves, has become a popular
summer resort, with windsurfing, snorkelling and
numerous discos. Many Germans have second homes
here; there have been complaints in the Mallorcan press
that it is becoming a 'German colony'.

A walk of about 2km from the harbour leads through
pine woods and crosses a headland to the lighthouse at
Punta de Capdepera, the easternmost point on Mallorca.
There are also several good beaches within easy reach.
The town beach, Son Moll, is often crowded but for more
isolation you can head north to the small cove of Cala Gat
or the broad sweep of Cala Agulla.

The other reason for coming here is to make a day trip
to Menorca (► 121). Fast boats leave each morning for
the Menorcan city of Ciutadella, with its Gothic cathedral
and harbourside fish restaurants.

28B3

Choice of restaurants and
bars (€€)

From Palma

Market held Mon

CALVIÀ ✪

Calvià is like an old lady who has won the *lotería* and
doesn't know how to cope with her success. Until recently
an unassuming country town, Calvià hit the jackpot when
tourists discovered the nearby beaches and it is now said
to be the richest municipality in Spain. There are a few

Tales of old Calvià in this ceramic display, created by local arts students to introduce visitors to the history of their town

ostentatious signs of wealth, like the sparkling new town hall and sports stadium, but mostly life continues as before, with ochre-coloured houses, a handful of shops and bars, and chickens scrambling between the olive trees. The town is dominated by the church of Sant Joan Baptista, built in the late 19th century around the 13th-century original; near here, by a fountain, a ceramic mural tells the story of Calvià's history. Founded in 1249 with 80 inhabitants, the town had a population of 3,000 in 1960 and 11,500 in 1980 – all because of tourism. Stand on the terrace looking out over almond and carob trees and it is hard to believe you are just a few kilometres from the teeming resorts of 'Maganova'.

CAMPOS ✪

Midway from Llucmajor to Santanyí on the C717, Campos was founded by Jaume II in 1300 on the site of earlier Roman and Arab settlements. A painting of Christ by the Sevillian artist Murillo hangs in the parish church of Sant Julià. Next door to the church is a museum with a large collection of offertory bowls. To visit both the church and the museum, meet the parish priest outside the church door at 11AM for a guided tour. Campos has a busy market on Thursdays and Saturdays and its port adjoins the resort of Colònia de Sant Jordi (► 51) to the south.

🔲 29D2
🍴 Several cafés and bars (€)
🚌 From Palma
❓ Market held Thu, Sat

Església de Sant Julià
✉ Carrer Bisbe Talladas 17
☎ 971 650003
🕐 Mon–Sat 11AM
💰 Donation requested

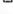 29F4

🍴 Café de l'Orient, Plaça de l'Orient (€)

🚌 From Palma and Cala Rajada

↔ Cala Rajada (➤ 48)

❓ Market held Wed; Nostra Senyora de la Esperança *festa*, 18 Dec

Castle

☎ 971 818746

🕐 Apr–Oct, daily 10–8; Nov–Mar, daily 10–5

💷 Cheap

✚ 28C2

✉ Carretera Cap Blanc–Llucmajor

☎ 971 180155

🕐 Fri–Wed 10–5

🍴 Near by (€)

💷 Cheap

Capdepera's castle dominates the views of the town as you approach

50

CAP DE FORMENTOR (➤ 18, TOP TEN)

CAPDEPERA ✪✪

If you are driving between Artà and Cala Rajada, stop off to visit this small town, crowned by the largest fortress in Mallorca. The Romans were the first to build a castle on this site – the Moors enlarged it, the Christians destroyed it, then replaced it with one of their own in the 14th century. Legend has it that the citizens of Capdepera hid in the castle when under siege, placing an image of Our Lady of Hope on the battlements, and the invaders were driven away by fog. The miracle is recorded inside the castle in the Capella de Nostra Senyora de la Esperança and remembered each year at the town's annual *festa*. You reach the castle by climbing the steps from the market square, Plaça de l'Orient.

CAPOCORB VELL ✪✪

These are the most significant remains of the Talaiotic culture, which flourished in Mallorca between around 1300 and 800 BC. Villages were dominated by *talaiots*, circular or rectangular structures two to three storeys high, which were used as both burial chambers and defensive forts. Each settlement was surrounded by Cyclopean walls, built from massive, unhewn stones without mortar to hold them together. There is no evidence of a written language, so the stones are all that archaeologists have to go on in understanding prehistoric Mallorcan culture. At Capocorb Vell, 12km south of Llucmajor, you can see five *talaiots* and wander around the ancient village, 100m above sea level just inland from the coast. The Talaiotic people kept sheep, and the sound of sheep bells in the nearby fields is a touching reminder of continuity.

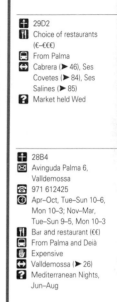

CASTELL D'ALARÓ (► 19, TOP TEN)

COLÒNIA DE SANT JORDI ✪

Once the port for the market town of Campos, Colònia de Sant Jordi is now a busy resort, on a rocky promontory close to Mallorca's southern tip. Its small beach looks out over several islets, with good views all the way to Cabrera (► 46). There are two further sandy beaches to the east, and the long stretch of Platja Es Trenc begins just west of town. To the north are the hot springs of Banys de Sant Joan. The main reason for coming here, though, is to take the boat trip to Cabrera.

✚ 29D2
🍴 Choice of restaurants
(€–€€€)
🚌 From Palma
🔁 Cabrera (► 46), Ses
Covetes (► 84), Ses
Salines (► 85)
❓ Market held Wed

COSTA NORD ✪✪

The American actor Michael Douglas could be seen as a 21st-century successor to Archduke Ludwig Salvator (► 88, 89), using his money and his influence to promote the landscapes and culture of Mallorca. In 2000 he opened Costa Nord, a multimedia cultural centre in Valldemossa devoted to Mallorca's north coast. The visit begins with a short film, narrated by Douglas, in which he describes his love for the island; it continues with a recreation of the Archduke's yacht, the *Nixe*, accompanied by a commentary on his Mediterranean voyages. The shop sells a range of pricey souvenirs; there is also a café, a restaurant and a concert hall which attracts top international names during the Mediterranean Nights festival each summer. Costa Nord is a personal tribute to an island which, as Douglas says, has attracted 'poets, painters... and yes, film stars'.

✚ 28B4
✉ Avinguda Palma 6,
Valldemossa
☎ 971 612425
🕐 Apr–Oct, Tue–Sun 10–6,
Mon 10–3; Nov–Mar,
Tue–Sun 9–5, Mon 10–3
🍴 Bar and restaurant (€€)
🚌 From Palma and Deià
✋ Expensive
🔁 Valldemossa (► 26)
❓ Mediterranean Nights,
Jun–Aug

*Watersports and sandy
beaches at Colònia de
Sant Jordi*

In the Know

If you only have a short time to visit Mallorca, or would like to get a real flavour of the island, here are some ideas:

Ways To Be A Local

Try to learn a little of the language, Catalan as well as Spanish – a simple *bon dia* goes a long way.

Relax, take your time and settle into the Mediterranean way of life.

Take a siesta to avoid the afternoon sun – have a long lunch, or rest in the shade.

Do everything late – a late lunch, a late supper, a very late night.

Join the evening *passeig* to see and be seen – put on your best clothes and pop into a bar for *tapas* and a chilled sherry.

Change out of your beachwear for restaurants, shops and churches – Mallorcans rarely dress formally but they always manage to look smart.

Find a local *festa* and get swept along with the crowd.

Go walking in the mountains at weekends, or join a *romeria* (pilgrimage) to a hilltop church.

Respect the local environment – don't drop litter or pick wild flowers.

Drink your coffee strong and sweet, with a touch of brandy, whatever the time of day.

Good Places To Have Lunch

Bon Lloc (€) ✉ Carrer Sant Feliu 7, Palma ☎ 971 718617. You won't find better value than this four-course vegetarian lunch. ◷ Closed Sun.

Ca N'Antuna (€€) ✉ Carrer Arbona Colom 7, Fornalutx ☎ 971 633068. Dine on a terrace overlooking the orange groves. ◷ Closed Mon.

Celler Sa Font (€€) ✉ Plaça d'Espanya 18,

Sineu ☎ 971 520313. Where the farmers go after Sineu's Wed market.

Centro (€) ✉ Avinguda Bisbe Campins 13, Porreres ☎ 971 168372. Huge portions, excellent food, ridiculous prices – in an old theatre. ◷ Closed Sun.

Es Verger (€€) ✉ On the way to Castell d'Alaró ☎ 971 182126. Farmhouse restaurant specialising in roast lamb from a wood-burning oven.

La Gran Tortuga (€€) ✉ Aldea Cala Fornells 1, Peguera ☎ 971 686023. Eat and swim on a terrace overlooking the sea. ◷ Closed Mon.

Puig de Sant Miquel (€€) ✉ Carretera de Manacor, km 31 ☎ 971 646314. Roast kid and other Mallorcan specialities beside a hilltop sanctuary near Montuïri.

Simple Fosh (€€) ✉ Read's Hotel, Santa Maria del Camí ☎ 971 140261 Marc Fosh turns out lighter, delicious bistro-style meals at lunchtime.

Stay (€€€) ✉ Moll Nou, Port de Pollença ☎ 971 864013.

Port de Sóller, seen from the Mirador de Ses Barques

Fresh fish harbourside.
Taberna de la Boveda
(€€) ✉ Passeig Sagrera 3,
Palma ☎ 971 720026.
Great *tapas* on the water-
front. ⊙ Closed Sun.

Top Activities

Birdwatching: the best
areas are the S'Albufera
wetlands, the salt flats
around Ses Salines, and
Gorg Blau and Cúber
reservoirs between Sóller
and Lluc.
Cricket: have a game with
the MCC – Magaluf Cricket
Club ☎ 971 233262.
Cycling: bike hire is
available in resorts.
Golf: there are 15 courses
(► 113).
Horse riding: several
centres have classes for all
abilities.
Sailing: more than 40
marinas. Yachts can be
chartered locally and from

most marinas. The national
sailing school is at
Avinguda Joan Miró, Cala
Major ☎ 971 402512.
Scuba diving: clubs in Port
d'Andratx, Port de Sóller
and elsewhere (► 114).
Swimming: plenty of
sandy beaches and
sheltered coves. Never go
into the sea if the red flag
is flying.
Walking: especially in the
Serra de Tramuntana. Take
a map, compass, sun hat
and plenty of water.
Windsurfing: equipment
can be hired at most of the
main resorts where there
are also schools giving
windsurfing lessons.

Good Beaches

- Cala Millor
- Es Trenc (nudist)
- Formentor
- Platja de Palma
- Port de Pollença

Best Viewpoints

- Castell d'Alaró
- Castell de Bellver
- Ermita de Bonany
- Mirador de Ses Animes,
  Banyalbufar
- Mirador de Ses Barques,
  Sóller–Lluc road
- Parc de la Mar, Palma
- Puig de Randa
- Puig de Santa Eugènia
- Puig de Teix, near Deià
- Santuari de Sant
  Salvador

Quiet Coves

- Cala de Deià
- Cala Torta (north of
  Artá)
- Cala Pi
- Cala Tuent (near Sa
  Calobra)
- Portals Vells

COVES D'ARTÀ (► 21, TOP TEN)

COVES DEL DRAC (DRAGON CAVES) ✪✪✪

Dank, dark and humid, these limestone caves on the edge of Porto Cristo have become one of Mallorca's top tourist sights. Groups of several hundred people at a time are herded along 2km of slippery paths by guides who tell you in four languages how to interpret the bizarre stalactite formations – a cactus here, a flag there, the Fairies' Theatre, Diana's Bath... You might just think they resemble thousands of spiky parsnips hanging from the ceiling. Try to imagine how Walt Disney would conjure up a fabulous witches' cave and you have the idea. The one-hour tour ends with a floodlit, floating violin concert on Lake Martel, Europe's largest underground lake, named after the French geologist Édouard Martel who first explored these caves in the late 19th century at the commission of Archduke Ludwig Salvator. Afterwards you can return by boat across the lake to the exit.

COVES DELS HAMS ✪✪

You cannot miss these caves as you drive from Manacor to Porto Cristo. Most people only want to visit one set of caves and the giant billboards and flags at the entrance are an attempt to ensure that this is the one. In fact you are better off continuing to the Coves del Drac (► above) or up the coast to the Coves d'Artà (► 21). But for serious speleologists, here are the facts. The caves were discovered by Pedro Caldentey in 1905 and the electric lighting was added by his son. Their name means 'fish-hooks', which the stalactites are said to resemble. You get a guided tour and, yes, another concert on an underground lake.

DEIÀ (► 22, TOP TEN)

Sidebar (Coves del Drac):

✛ 29E3
☎ 971 820753
🕓 Apr–Oct, tours on the hour 10–5; Nov–Mar, tours at 10:45, 12, 2, 3:30
🍴 Café (€)
🚌 From Palma and Cala Rajada
♿ None
💰 Expensive
🔁 Porto Cristo (► 74), Coves dels Hams (► below), Acuàrium de Mallorca (► 109)

Sidebar (Coves dels Hams):

✛ 29E3
✉ Carretera Manacor–Porto Cristo
☎ 971 820988
🕓 Apr–Oct, daily 10–6; Nov–Mar, daily 11–4:30
🍴 Café-restaurant (€)
♿ None
💰 Expensive
🔁 Porto Cristo (► 74), Coves del Drac (► above)

ERMITA DE BONANY ✪✪

This hilltop hermitage is where Junípero Serra preached his last sermon in Mallorca before leaving to found the Mexican and Californian missions. The views from the terrace, covering almost the entire plain, are superb. You can stay here in simple cells, but unlike other monasteries it has no restaurant or bar – just a chapel and a small shop selling religious trinkets.

➕ 29D3
☎ 971 561101
🎫 Free
↔ Petra (▶ 64)

> ### Did you know ?
>
> Bon any *means good year.*
> *The first church was built here in 1604; five years later,*
> *during a drought, the villagers of Petra*
> *climbed to the chapel to pray for rain. When their*
> *prayers were answered with a* bon any, *they named*
> *their sanctuary Bonany.*

FELANITX ✪

Felanitx is at the centre of Mallorca's second wine-producing area and it is also known for its capers, or 'green pearls'. You can buy them at the Sunday morning market, which spills out onto the streets around the church of Sant Miquel, with local pottery displayed on the church steps. The church façade contains a memorial to 414 people who died when a wall collapsed in 1844; further up, beneath the rose window, you can see the archangel Michael standing on the Devil's head.

➕ 29E3
🍴 Bars and cafés (£)
🚌 From Palma and Porto Colom
↔ Santuari de Sant Salvador (▶ 82)
❓ Market held Sun; Sant Agusti, *cavallets* horse dances, 28 Aug

FORNALUTX ✪✪

Fornalutx, in the hills above Sóller, calls itself the prettiest village in Spain, and it is hard to disagree – unless you accept the claims of its neighbour Biniaraix. There are several terrace restaurants and bars, where you can sit and soak in the views of olive and orange groves climbing ever higher until they reach the pine-clad foothills of Puig Major.

➕ 28C4
🍴 Several restaurants (££)
↔ Sóller (▶ 86)

The prettiest village in Spain? Go and judge for yourself

🏛 72B2
✉ Carrer Joan de Saridakis
   29, Cala Major
☎ 971 701420
🕐 15 May–15 Sep, Tue–Sat
   10–7, Sun 10–3; 16 Sep–
   14 May, Tue–Sat 10–6,
   Sun 10–3
🍴 Café (€)
🚌 6 from Palma
♿ Good
Ⓜ Moderate

FUNDACIÓ PILAR I JOAN MIRÓ ✪✪

The painter and sculptor Joan Miró spent most of his life in Barcelona, but both his wife and mother were Mallorcan and he always longed to return to the scene of his childhood holidays to draw inspiration from what he called 'the light of Mallorca'. In 1956, aged 63, he bought a house and studio in Cala Major. He lived here until he died in 1983 after which it was enlarged to hold a permanent exhibition of his works.

The collection includes more than 100 paintings, 25 sculptures and 3,000 studio pieces but only a small amount is displayed at any time. The paintings are almost childish, all vivid splashes of bright primary colours, influenced by his love of peasant traditions and his fascination with *siurells* (clay whistles). Anyone tempted to remark that their child could do better should take a look at the heavily realistic work that Miró was producing aged eight – the fantasy came later. Works on display include the draft for UNESCO's *Mural del Sol* in Paris.

Glance into Miró's studio, left untouched since his death, with work in progress, open tins of paint and black stains all over the floor.

The Wind amongst the Bulrushes *by Joan Miró (1971)*

🏛 28B3
🍴 Two bars (€)
↔ La Reserva (▶ 76)

GALILEA ✪✪

This pretty village, 460m above sea level, in the shadow of the great peak of Puig de Galatzó, gets crowded out by day trippers who come to sample the views from the church terrace. On a good day you can see far out to sea, while eating *tapas* outside the church and listening to the echo of sheep-bells on the hillsides. The nearby village of Puigpunyent is also justifiably popular and is surrounded by orange groves – as well as being the base for visiting La Reserva (▶ 76).

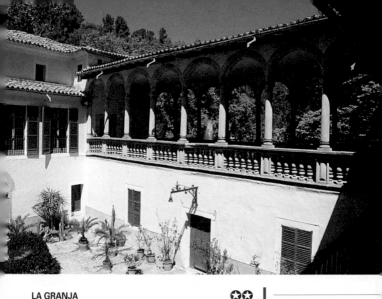

LA GRANJA ✪✪

This country house, just south of Banyalbufar, is on a site known since Roman times for its natural spring. When Jaume I conquered Mallorca he divided the island into four feudal estates, giving one to Count Nuno Sanç, who settled at La Granja. In 1239 the Count handed the estate to Cistercian monks to found Mallorca's first monastery. Since 1447 it has been a private house owned by various noble families; most of what you see today dates from the 17th century.

Highlights of the tour include an aristocratic drawing-room with its own theatre, the family chapel and a dungeon with a torture chamber – but the real reason for visiting La Granja is to learn about rural Mallorcan traditions. Workshops, cellars and kitchens contain displays of everyday objects. And on Wednesday and Friday afternoons, women in traditional costume give demonstrations of lacemaking, embroidery and spinning, donkeys turn threshing-wheels and there are tastings of cheese, wine, sausages, doughnuts and fig cake. Look carefully and you just might see a tray of *coca* (Mallorcan pizza) being removed from the restaurant oven and carried to the medieval kitchens to be served beside a log fire. There are also displays of bagpipe music and folk dancing, which are entertaining if not terribly authentic.

Escape from the tour groups by walking in the grounds, which contain botanical gardens, waterfalls and a thousand-year-old yew – there is a 1,200-m signed walk. La Granja is still a working farm and you may see pigs, turkeys, chickens and goats as well as displays of agricultural implements and tools.

If you have not gorged yourself on free samples, the restaurant serves good Mallorcan staples like *pa amb oli* and *sopes mallorquines*.

✚ 28B4
☎ 971 610032
🕑 Apr–Sep, daily 10–7;
   Oct–Mar, daily 10–6
🍴 Restaurant (€)
🚍 From Palma
♿ None
💰 Expensive
↔ Banyalbufar (➤ 46)
❓ Folk fiesta, Wed, Fri
   3:30–5

The estate at La Granja has been turned into a living museum, where staff dressed in folk costume give displays of Mallorcan traditions

INCA ✪

Mallorca's third-largest town styles itself 'city of leather', and if you come on an organised tour you will undoubtedly be taken to a leather factory. Shop around; the bargains these days are few and far between. Better to come on Thursdays, when the streets around Plaça d'Espanya are taken over by Mallorca's largest weekly market. Plenty of leather here, of varying quality, plus jewellery, carved olive-wood, lace and fresh produce from across the island. Plaça d'Espanya itself becomes an open-air flower show. Near here are a smart coffee-house, Café Mercantil, with uphol-stered leather chairs, and Ca'n Delante (✉ Carrer Major 27), one of Mallorca's top pastry shops. Inca is also known for its *cellers*, old wine-cellars turned into restaurants featuring traditional dishes at reasonable prices.

JARDINS DE ALFÁBIA ✪✪

These classical gardens by the entrance to the Sóller tunnel are a legacy of the Arab talent for landscaping and irrigation. Their name derives from *al fabi*, 'jar of olives' in Arabic. They were probably designed by Benihabet, the Muslim governor of Inca who converted to Christianity following the Spanish invasion.

A flight of steps lined with tall palms leads to a covered walkway – from here you can strike off to see lily ponds, bamboo groves or citrus trees growing in the shadow of the mountains. If you have just driven over the Coll de Sóller and are in need of a rest, this would make a lovely spot for a siesta. Take a book or some postcards, find a seat in the shade, then drift off to sleep to the sound of gently flowing water.

LLUC (➤ 23, TOP TEN)

LLUC-ALCARI ✪

You could easily miss Mallorca's smallest village, which consists of little more than a bend in the Deià–Sóller road. With just a handful of houses and a hotel, it would make an ideal base for a walking holiday in the nearby mountains. The views are postcard-perfect – in fact you are far more likely to see it on a postcard than you are to actually go there. Picasso once lived in the village during a short stay on Mallorca.

LLUCMAJOR

This ordinary country town, the largest in southern Mallorca, has a place in history – it was the site of the battle in 1349 where Pedro IV of Aragón killed his relative Jaume III to end Mallorca's brief spell as an independent kingdom. Jaume's death is commemorated by a statue at the end of Passeig Jaume III. Near by, on Carrer Obispo Taxaquet, is another statue in honour of Llucmajor's cobblers. Shoemaking is still a significant industry here. Almonds and apricots grow around the town and make good buys at the market, held twice a week in Plaça d'Espanya.

28C3
Cafés and bars (€)
From Palma
Puig de Randa (➤ 75)
Market held Wed, Sun

MAGALUF

More than anywhere else in Mallorca, Magaluf has been blighted by the curse of mass tourism. During the 1980s it became a byword for all that was wrong with Mallorca; foreign TV crews would flock here to film drinking competitions, wet T-shirt contests and teenagers throwing up on the beach. However, in the 1990s Magaluf tried hard to change its image. High-rise hotels have been destroyed, a new seafront promenade has been built, and the council has introduced activities from guided walks to *tai chi* on the beach. But still the lager louts come... and if you want cheap sun, sea, sand and *sangría*, there's no better place.

28B3
Huge choice of bars and restaurants (€)
Regular buses from Palma
Palma Nova (➤ 63), Portals Vells (➤ 72)

Magaluf – never mind the lager louts, the beach is superb

➕ 29E3

🍽 Several bars and cafés (€)

🚌 From Palma and Porto Cristo

❓ Market held Mon

Perlas Majórica

✉ Avinguda Majórica 48

☎ 971 550200

🕐 Mon–Fri 9–7, Sat–Sun 10–1

🎫 Free

Setting pearls into their gold surrounds at a factory in Manacor

---

MANACOR ⭐

Mallorca's second city is the nearest thing the island has to an industrial town. Despite the lack of obvious sights, the narrow streets behind the church make a pleasant place to stroll and soak up the atmosphere of everyday Mallorca. The church, Església dels Delors de Nostra Senyora, was built on the site of a mosque and its minaret-style tower can be seen for miles. Look inside to see the figure of Christ with scrawny hair and a skirt – pilgrims queue up to kiss his bloodstained feet.

Almost every visitor to Manacor ends up at a pearl factory – **Perlas Majórica** is the best-known. Mallorca's artificial pearl industry produces 50 million pearls a year, using the scales of a million fish, so do not imagine they are a safe alternative for your vegetarian friends. They are said to be indistinguishable from the real thing, and almost as expensive.

➕ 29D3

🍽 Restaurants and bars (€)

🚌 From Palma

🔁 Algaida (▶ 43), Vilafranca de Bonany (▶ 90)

❓ Market held Mon; Sant Bartomeu festival, 24 Aug; Fira de la Perdiu (partridge and hunting fair), first Sun in Dec

---

MONTUÏRI ⭐

High on a ridge surrounded by old stone windmills, the village of Montuïri is probably the most impressive sight along the Palma–Manacor road. The eight mill-towers of the Molinar district, redundant since the 1920s, are the symbol of the village; the best views are from the Ermita de Sant Miquel, a 19th-century hermitage on top of a small hill 2km to the east. Montuïri is the setting for one of Mallorca's most spectacular festivals: each August *Cossiers*, accompanied by dancers with bagpipes, flutes and drums, dress up as women and devils and perform a dance, the origins of which stretch back at least 400 years, where evil is overcome by good.

The Northeast

This leisurely half-day drive takes in several family attractions close to the northeast coast. It can easily be done as a day trip from Palma, adding 1½ hours to the time.

Begin by the OlivArt factory shop, as you enter Manacor on the C715 from Palma. Follow signs to Porto Cristo, leaving Manacor along a boulevard with palm trees down the middle.

After 13km you see the Coves dels Hams (▶ 54) – choose between stopping here or continuing to Porto Cristo for the Coves del Drac (▶ 54).

Take the bypass around Porto Cristo, or drive down to the seafront, where you turn left up a steep hill, following signs to Cala Millor.

A word in your ear – you never know who you might meet on a drive around Safari-Zoo

The road leads through orchards divided by drystone walls, reaching Safari-Zoo (▶ 45), where you can drive around the zoo.

Continue north, bypassing Cala Millor to arrive in Son Servera. Turn right towards Capdepera (▶ 50).

Long before you get there you see the castle crowning the village on a hill. Stop here for lunch and a climb to the castle, then if you feel like an afternoon on the beach take the side road to Cala Mesquida.

Otherwise take the C715 to Artà.

After exploring Artà (▶ 45), take to the coast.

Follow the C712 coast road around the bay of Alcúdia, with the dark silhouette of Cap de Formentor looming up ahead of you.

You pass Ca'n Picafort and the S'Albufera nature reserve (▶ 77) before finally reaching Alcúdia (▶ 16).

Return to Palma in under an hour by taking the C713 and joining the motorway at Inca.

Distance
80km

Time
4 hours including visits to a cave and the zoo

Start point
Manacor
✚ 29E3

End point
Alcúdia
✚ 29D5

Lunch
Café l'Orient (€)
✉ Plaça de l'Orient, Capdepera
☎ 971 563098

61

29D4

Sun market; Revelta de Sant Antoni, 16–17 Jan

Train from Palma

Museu Etnòlogic de Mallorca

Carrer Major 15

971 860647

Tue–Sat 10–3, Sun 10–2; also Thu 5–8

Cheap

Revealing Mallorca's past

MURO ✪✪

This small town between Inca and the S'Albufera marshes has one overriding attraction – the **Museu Etnòlogic de Mallorca**. This museum, housed in a former mansion, gives fascinating glimpses into Mallorca's past. The kitchen contains pottery similar to what you see in the markets today; the recreated pharmacy has a pair of scales in the shape of a crucifix. Upstairs there is a fine collection of *siurells* (clay whistles) featuring men on horseback, carrying water and playing guitars. A courtyard with a well, a waterwheel and orange trees leads to more exhibits – blacksmith's and cobbler's workshops, a collection of carriages, and tools once used by silversmiths, sculptors and spoonmakers.

The Catalan-Gothic church of Sant Joan Baptista looks almost Arabic, guarded by palm trees and a tall, square bell-tower linked to the main church by a tiny bridge. Rebuilt in the 16th century, it has a colourful rose window over the west door. Another church, the convent of Santa Anna, used to stage fights between bulls and bulldogs, and bullfights can still be seen at the Plaça de Toros, built out of white stone in its own quarry in 1910.

Sa Pobla, 4km north of Muro, is Mallorca's vegetable basket; this fertile area of marshes reclaimed as farmland is referred to as 'the land of a thousand windmills'. It is also the home of one of Mallorca's most unusual festivals, the Revelta de Sant Antoni. For two days each January pets are led through the town to be blessed outside the church, dancers drive out the Devil for the coming year, and everyone eats pastries filled with spicy spinach and marsh eels.

ORIENT

Nervous drivers should not even think about tackling the 10-km hairpin road to Orient from Bunyola (there is a much easier approach from Alaró). But those who make it to this village are rewarded with a marvellous sight – one of Mallorca's tiniest hamlets, with a population of less than 30, nestling among olive trees at the foot of Puig d'Alfábia. Orient is popular with walkers – numerous walks start from here, including an ascent to Castell d'Alaró – and with weekend day trippers from Palma, who visit its three restaurants for Sunday lunch.

✚ 28C4
🍴 Three good restaurants (€€)
🔄 Castell d'Alaró (► 19)

Orient is a favourite spot for mountain walkers, cyclists and lovers of Mallorcan cuisine

PALMA NOVA

There are people who can remember when this was just a village; then along came the tourist boom, and 'new Palma' became the favoured resort of the British. More restrained than Magaluf, less exclusive than Portals Nous, Palma Nova occupies a prime position on the western side of the bay of Palma. It makes a good base for a family holiday, with nearby attractions including Marineland and Aquapark (► 108, 109) – as long as you don't mind sharing your family holiday with a thousand others.

✚ 28B3
🍴 Wide choice of restaurants (€–€€)
🚌 Regular buses from Palma
🔄 Magaluf (► 59), Portals Nous (► 72)

PEGUERA

This beach resort, popular with German tour operators, was the first in Mallorca to have its own artificial beach. Once on the main road from Palma to Andratx, it has become much more peaceful since the construction of a bypass and the opening of a seafront promenade. Just outside Peguera is Cala Fornells, a chic resort of terracotta houses set around a pretty cove. Nearby Camp de Mar is a fast-growing resort where racing driver Michael Schumacher and model Claudia Schiffer both have homes.

✚ 28B3
🍴 Wide choice of restaurants (€–€€)
🚌 From Palma

The house in Petra where Junípero Serra was born has been preserved much as it would have been in the 18th century

+ 29D3
🍴 Es Celler restaurant (€€); bars on main square (€)
🚂 Train from Palma
🔁 Ermita de Bonany (▶ 55)
❓ Market held Wed

Serra House and Museum
✉ Carrer Barracar Alt
☎ 971 561149
🕐 By arrangement – follow the directions to the keyholder's house
 Donation requested

+ 73C2
🍴 Wide choice of bars and restaurants (€–€€)
🚌 Regular buses from Palma

PETRA ⚫⚫

This sleepy town of sand-coloured houses would be completely off the tourist map if it were not the birthplace of Mallorca's most famous son, Fray Junípero Serra. Born in 1713, he became a priest in 1730 and worked as a missionary in Mexico from 1749 to 1763. At the age of 54 he was sent to California; the missions he established there grew into some of the USA's largest cities, including San Diego and San Francisco.

You can visit the house where Serra's parents lived, a museum devoted to his life and work, the nearby San Bernardino convent where he went to school and a plaque, outside the parish church, describing him as 'explorer, missionary, hero, civiliser'. Anyone walking down the street leading to his birthplace, decorated with majolica tiles depicting him baptising Native Americans, might be inclined to disagree, but by the standards of his day he was certainly a hero.

PLATJA DE PALMA ⚫

If you cannot wait to get on a beach, this 5-km stretch of fine white sand is just minutes from the airport. The two resorts of Can Pastilla and S'Arenal have merged into one, connected by a long palm-lined promenade offering every possible entertainment in summer. This is a good resort for families – there are children's playgrounds and a miniature train ride, though the nightlife can get a bit raucous. Take a *passeig* here before dinner and you have a fabulous view of Palma, the twinkling lights on the water-front reflected in the sea.

The Central Plain

This lovely drive criss-crosses the central plain (Es Pla), following old Roman roads through almond and apricot groves and vineyards on its way to a number of small market towns.

Start in Petra by the parish church, following signs to Felanitx. On the way out of the village, you pass the road leading up to Ermita de Bonany (▶ 55), where the views are splendid across the plain.

Keep straight ahead at a roundabout to cross over the C715, the main road from Palma to Manacor. Stay on this country road for 7km, then turn left towards Felanitx (▶ 55). When you see the town ahead of you, take a sharp right turn, signposted to Porreres.

Follow this road across fertile countryside for 12km and into the centre of Porreres (▶ 67), which is a good place to stop for lunch with its numerous bars and cafés.

Leaving Porreres, follow signs to Llucmajor. Stay on this road for 12km as farmland gradually gives way to woods. Reaching Llucmajor (▶ 59) – with its Wednesday and Saurday market – turn left at the roundabout and stay on the ring road to the far end of town, where you turn right, following signs to Algaida.

The road rises and falls for 8km around the foot of Puig de Randa (▶ 75), a highlight of Mallorca with its sense of history and religious connotations. When you reach Algaida (▶ 43), turn right to briefly join the C715 to Manacor. After 1km, turn left towards Pina and stay on this pretty rural road through Pina and Lloret de Vistalegre, with views of the sierra in the distance as you head towards Sineu (▶ 86). Here you can visit the modern art gallery, S'Estació, located in an old station.

Just before entering Sineu (come on a Wednesday morning for one of Mallorca's most traditional markets), turn right to skirt the town centre and turn right again to return to Petra on the old road.

Distance
80km

Time
2 hours

Start/end point
Petra
✚ 29D3

Lunch
Centro (€)
✉ Avinguda Bisbe Campins, Porreres
☎ 971 168372

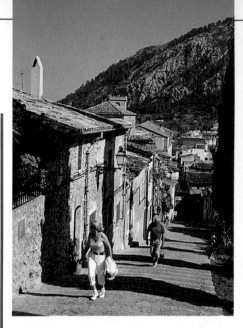

Climbing the Calvari steps on the way to salvation, with Puig de Maria in the background

➕ 29D5
🍴 Excellent cafés and restaurants (€€)
🚌 From Palma
↔️ Cala de Sant Vicenç (➤ 47), Port de Pollença (➤ 70), Puig de Maria (➤ 74)
❓ Market held Sun; classical music festival, Jul–Sep; *Devallement* procession, Good Fri; *Moros i Cristians*, mock battle, 2 Aug

Museu de Pollença
✉️ Carrer Guillem Cifre de Colonya
☎️ 971 531166
🕐 Jul–Sep, Tue–Sat 10–1, 5:30–8:30, Sun–10–1; Oct–Jun, Tue–Sun 11–1
💰 Cheap

POLLENÇA ✪✪✪

At the eastern end of the Serra de Tramuntana and tucked between two hills, each topped by a sacred site, Pollença is the perfect Mallorcan town. Large enough to avoid being twee but small enough to wander round in a morning, it has none of the feel of other towns which have succumbed under the sheer weight of tourism. Foreigners have long been attracted here, but Pollença has learned to accept and adapt to tourism without losing its soul. Café life is still the rule; if you want to join in, come on a Sunday morning when the Plaça Major is filled with market stalls and the locals congregate after church to relax in the Café Espanyol.

The Pont Romà (Roman bridge) on the edge of town gives a clue to Pollença's long history. The name Pollença dates from the 14th century, when settlers from Alcúdia named the town after their former Roman capital. Among many historic buildings is a former Jesuit convent, now the town hall. From here you climb 365 steps, lined with cypress trees, to reach the Calvari church, with its ancient wooden cross and views of Puig de Maria (➤ 74). The Calvari steps are the scene of a moving procession each Good Friday, when a figure of Christ is removed from a cross and carried down the steps by torchlight.

The **municipal museum** in the former Dominican convent contains the remains of prehistoric sculptures shaped like bulls, as well as a *mandala* (Tibetan sand painting) given by the Dalai Lama in 1990. The cloisters of the convent are the venue for Pollença's celebrated classical music festival.

PORRERES ✪

Porreres is typical of the small towns on the Mallorcan plain – nothing much to see, but an easy-going atmosphere and a good place to while away a couple of hours. The main street, Avinguda Bisbe Campins, runs from the church to the town hall and is lined with bars and cafés. A former hospital contains the **Museu i Fons Artistic**, which opened in 2002 and features works by Salvador Dalí. Just outside Porreres is a former hilltop hermitage, Santuari de Montesió, with a simple chapel, irregular cloisters and views across the plain and out to sea.

🔢 29D3
🍴 Choice of restaurants and bars (€)
❓ Market held Tue

Museu i Fons Artistic
✉ Carrer Augustí Font 23
☎ 971 166617
🕐 Tue, Thu & Sat 11–1
🎟 Free

PORT D'ALCÚDIA ✪

As the name suggests, this was once just a port serving a city – now the port has completely outgrown the town that it serves. The biggest of the resorts on Mallorca's northeast coast, it stands at the head of a 10-km stretch of sandy beach which continues around the bay of Alcúdia as far as Can Picafort. The area around the fishing harbour is the most attractive; the promenade on Passeig Marítim faces a row of fish restaurants. Near here is the commercial port, where passenger ferries leave for the Menorcan city of Ciutadella.

🔢 29D5
🍴 Wide choice of restaurants (€€)
🚌 From Palma and Alcúdia; also from Port de Pollença in summer
↔ Alcúdia (➤ 16)

PORT D'ANDRATX ✪✪

Dress up to come here, or you will feel seriously out of place. Port d'Andratx is one of Mallorca's classiest resorts, popular with the yachting fraternity and with film stars whose Italian-style villas can be seen climbing up the hillsides. But don't let that put you off; come here all the same. The harbour is one of the prettiest in Mallorca and a table at one of the waterside bars is really the perfect place to watch the sunset.

🔢 28A3
🍴 Wide choice of restaurants (€€–€€€)
🚌 From Andratx
↔ Andratx (➤ 43)

Port d'Andratx, where the yachting set like to meet

Food & Drink

Mallorcan cuisine, based on pork, fish and vegetables with generous use of garlic and olive oil, is hearty peasant fare steeped in tradition and rooted in local ingredients.

Good *Tapas*
- *Datiles con bacon* – dates wrapped in bacon
- *Mejillones relleñas* – stuffed mussels
- *Pimientos de Padrón* – small chillies deep-fried with salt
- *Pulpo gallego* – Galician-style octopus with olive oil
- *Tortilla española* – cold potato omelette

Not long ago every village would celebrate the *matança*, the winter slaughter of pigs, with songs and dancing and the making of hams and sausages for the coming year. Sausages come in several varieties – *sobrasada* (raw minced pork with hot red pepper) and *botifarró* (cured pork with blood), as well as spicy *chorizo* from Spain. And no bar would be complete without its *jamón serrano*, a whole cured ham displayed on an attractive slicing-board.

Mallorcan Specialities

A side effect of the *matança* was *frit mallorquí*, a fry-up of the most perishable offal with potatoes, onions and tomatoes. Nowadays you find it on menus alongside *tumbet*, a Mallorcan-style ratatouille of aubergines, potatoes and peppers in olive oil, and *sopes mallorquines*, a thick broth of thinly-sliced brown bread and vegetables. Other classic dishes include *llom amb col* (pork wrapped in cabbage with pine nuts and raisins) and *lechona asada* (roast suckling pig).

Paella is not a Mallorcan dish but it is widely available; *paella ciega* (blind man's *paella*) comes without bones. The local equivalent is *arròs brut* ('dirty rice'), saffron rice cooked with chicken, pork and vegetables. Fish is mostly imported and frozen – restaurants have to state this – but lobster, prawns, sardines and sea bass are all good. The latter, baked in rock salt, is a Mallorcan speciality.

Desserts are not Mallorca's strong point – often the choice is between *helado* (ice cream) and *flan* (crème caramel). . An interesting alternative is *gato de almendras*, almond cake served with toasted almond ice cream. Mallorcans are very proud of *ensaimadas*, fluffy,

spiral-shaped
pastries dusted with sugar and filled
with anything from pumpkin jam to
sobrasada sausage; the secret ingre-
dient is said to be the lard in the pastry.
Cheeses include Mahón from Menorca and
Manchego from central Spain as well as local varieties.

Sobrasada *sausages
(above) and* ensaimadas
*(left) are treated with a
reverence normally
reserved for works of art*

Wine

The *vi* or *vino de la casa* will probably be Mallorcan, but
most bottled wine is imported from Spain. The best red
wines come from La Rioja – wine labelled *crianza* is aged
in oak for at least a year, *reserva* for two, *gran reserva* for
three. Penedés red and white wines from Catalunya are
good value; Cava, Spanish sparkling wine, is from the
same area. But don't disparage Mallorcan wines – the best
stand comparison with anything at the same cost from
mainland Spain (▶ 107).

Other Alcoholic Drinks

Spanish and imported beer (*cerveza*) are available everywhere – for draught beer, ask for *una caña*. Sherry is
always *fino* – dry and chilled. Spanish brandy (*coñac*)
comes in a bewildering variety of bottles and is added to
coffee at any time of day. Leading brands include
Fundador, Magno and Soberano. Gin is manufactured on
Menorca – ask for Xoriguer brand. Local liqueurs include
hierbas secos (dry) and *hierbas dulces* (sweet), both based
on aniseed and packed full of herbs.

Soft Drinks

Tap water is safe but everyone drinks mineral water – *con
gas* is sparkling, *sin gas* is still. Freshly squeezed orange
juice (*zumo de naranja*) is refreshing and delicious, as are
summer *granizados* (fruit slushes) of orange or lemon. An
unusual local drink is *orxata* or *horchata*, almond milk. *Café
solo* is a small shot of strong black coffee; *café con leche*
comes with hot milk. If you want something less
stimulating, ask for *manzanilla* (camomile) or *poliomenta*
(peppermint tea).

29D5

🍴 Choice of restaurants (€)

🚌 From Palma, Pollença and Alcúdia; also from Port d'Alcúdia and Cap de Formentor in summer

↔ Alcúdia (► 16), Cala de Sant Vicenç (► 47), Cap de Formentor (► 18), Pollença (► 66)

❓ Market held Wed

PORT DE POLLENÇA ✪✪

This genteel, old-fashioned resort at the mouth of Pollença bay is particularly popular with families, and with older visitors in winter. There is also a large community of foreign residents, mostly retired British. The promenade along Passeig Voramar, all whitewashed villas and pine trees leaning into the sea, is perfect for an early evening walk. Look out for the bust of Hermen Anglada-Camarasa, the Catalan painter who spent many years in Pollença and whose work is displayed in the Fundació la Caixa in Palma (► 33). A favourite walk from Port de Pollença is the 3-km hike across the Formentor peninsula through the Bóquer valley, a paradise for ornithologists and lovers of wild flowers.

> ### Did you know ?
>
> Port de Pollença has long been the favoured resort of the British middle classes, who would stay at its water-front hotels enjoying casual flirtations and games of bowls on the beach. The British crime writer Agatha Christie captures this world in a 1936 short story, Problem at Pollensa Bay.

PORT DE SÓLLER ✪✪

This small resort, set around a fish-shaped natural harbour, has the only beach of any note along the entire north coast. It is the starting-point for several boat trips along the coast; the trip to Sa Calobra (► 78) is one of the few to run throughout the year. Port de Sóller is also a good base for walks. A climb of less than an hour brings you to Cap Gros lighthouse for panoramic views of the bay and the mountains behind; a longer path, through rock gardens and olive groves, connects with an old mule track from Deià to Sóller.

28C5

🍴 Wide choice of restaurants (€–€€€)

🚌 From Palma, Valldemossa and Deià

🚃 From Palma; tram from Sóller

↔ Sóller (► 86)

A Day Out by Train & Tram

The opening of a railway line from Palma to Sóller in 1912, and a tram linking Sóller to its port the following year, brought the northwest coast within easy reach of the capital. The vintage carriages are still in use, providing a joyride for tourists and a relief for locals from the terrors of the Palma–Sóller road. Five trains a day leave from Plaça d'Espanya in Palma – the 10:50 is labelled the *turistico* but all you get for the extra cost is a more crowded train and a short photo stop.

Time
1½ hours each way

Start point
Plaça d'Espanya, Palma
🗺 35D4
🚌 Most city buses terminate here; island buses terminate near by

End point
Port de Sóller
🗺 28C5

Lunch
Café Sóller (€)
✉ Plaça Constitució, Sóller
☎ 971 630010

The train, all mahogany panels and brass fittings, leaves Palma amid a bustle of hisses, hoots and whistles before rattling down the city streets and into the suburbs.

Soon you are out on the plain, passing small country stations and pigs rooting beneath the trees. If you feel like a break, you can get off at Bunyola and climb up the hill to reach the centre of this sleepy village, with cafés on the main square.

Stay on the train and soon you start to climb, entering a 3-km tunnel before returning to daylight for the drop, through a dizzying series of bends, to Sóller (➤ 86).

The 'Orange Express' tram to Port de Sóller runs hourly, connecting with the arrival of the train. Stand on the platform as it clatters through orchards and back gardens and you can imagine you are living 50 years earlier.

Take the toytown train from Palma to Sóller (above), then hop on a tram to its port (left)

It takes 20 minutes to complete the 5-km journey to the port. If you do not want to return the same way, there are regular express buses returning to Palma via the Sóller tunnel.

BADIA DE PALMA

72B2
Wide choice of bars and restaurants (€€–€€€)

From Palma

Palma Nova (► 63), Ses Illetes (► 85)

PORTALS NOUS ✪

This is one of the more exclusive resorts in the bay of Palma – not many high-rise hotels here, just rows of private villas and apartments dominating the shoreline. Puerto Portals marina, opened in 1987, is the summer home of the jet set. King Juan Carlos has been known to moor here while staying at his summer palace, Marivent, in nearby Cala Major, and the younger royals can be seen frequenting the waterfront restaurants and bars. Don't even think about looking in the smart boutiques unless you have a high credit card limit.

28B3
Beach bar and restaurant (€€)

From Palma Oct–May, Mon–Fri (☎ 971 717190)

PORTALS VELLS ✪✪

A bumpy track from Magaluf leads through pine woods to this beautiful cove at the southwest tip of Palma bay. In summer it gets crowded, but out of season you could have your own private beach, with golden sand, rocky cliffs and shimmering turquoise water. In fact there are two beaches; the smaller one, El Mago, is Mallorca's official nudist beach. From the main beach, hike along the cliffs to the Cove de la Mare de Déu, a rock chapel built by fishermen to give thanks for a safe landing. Back on the road, another 2km brings you to the headland of Cap de

Cala Figuera, where you look back at sweeping views of the entire bay of Palma.

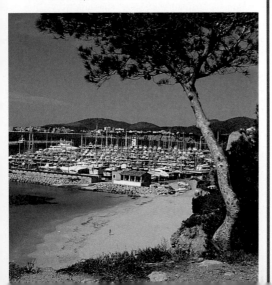

How the other half lives – the glitzy marina at Puerto Portals looks across the water to the mass-market resorts at Palma Nova and Magaluf

73

29E2
Choice of restaurants (€€)
From Palma and Felanitx

PORTO COLOM ✪

This fishing village, once the port for Felanitx, was named in honour of Christopher Columbus, who is said – without much evidence – to have been born here. Until the late 19th century Porto Colom was busy supplying wine to France; but when phylloxera killed the vines, its role as a port diminished and it has only recently discovered a new life as a tourist resort. Popular with Mallorcan and Spanish visitors and set inside a deep natural harbour, it still has the feel of a small fishing port with boats around the quay and pastel-coloured houses lining the waterfront, each with its own landing stage. Cala Marçal, 2km south, has a wide sandy beach leading to a narrow rocky cove.

29E3
Wide choice of
restaurants (€€)
From Palma and Manacor
Coves del Drac and
Coves dels Hams (► 54)
Market held Sun

PORTO CRISTO ✪

This was one of the main resorts on the east coast until Cala Millor came along. So much the better: with bigger and better beaches elsewhere, Porto Cristo has carved out a role as a friendly, family resort, taking advantage of a superb position at the end of a long, sheltered inlet. Once the port for Manacor, Porto Cristo was the only place in Mallorca to be caught up in the Spanish Civil War, when it was briefly captured by Republican forces in 1936. There is not much to do but swim, sunbathe and dine at the terrace restaurants which are perfectly placed to catch the lunchtime sun – but day trippers come in droves to visit the nearby caves (► 54). Other nearby family attractions include an aquarium and a safari park (► 108, 109).

28C4
Bars (€)
From Palma
Market held Thu; Fira del
Fang, annual pottery fair
held in Mar in the nearby
town of Marratxí

PÒRTOL ✪

The neighbouring villages of Pòrtol and Sa Cabaneta, between Palma and Santa Maria del Camí, have become something of an artists' colony. Unlike in Deià and Banyalbufar, though, the artists are Mallorcan – potters taking advantage of the rich local soil. The only reason for coming here is to visit the *ollerías* (workshops), where prices are much lower than in the tourist shops. Good buys include *greixoneras* (heavy earthenware cooking pots) and *ollas* (clay storage jars), as well as simple brown-glazed plates and *plats morenos*, glazed bowls painted with symbols (some of the designs go back to Arab times). Several artists specialise in the clay whistles called *siurells*.

29D5
971 184132
Bar-restaurant (€)
From Palma to Pollença
Free
Pollença (► 66)

PUIG DE MARIA ✪✪

Climb for an hour out of Pollença, or drive up a terrifying potholed road, and you are rewarded with views over Cap de Formentor and the entire northeastern coast – as well as back down over Pollença. Nuns settled on Puig de Maria ('Mary's mountain') in 1371 and remained for several hundred years, refusing to leave even when the Bishop of Palma ordered them down for their own safety. The convent is still there, on top of the mountain; the chapel smells of incense and the refectory of woodsmoke. You can stay in simple cells in the sanctuary here, but don't expect luxury – unless you count waking to a view of sunrise over Pollença Bay. The caretaker will rustle up a *paella* to save you the long walk back to town.

PUIG DE RANDA ✪✪✪

This table mountain, rising 543m out of the plain, has been a place of pilgrimage ever since Ramón Llull (► 14) founded Mallorca's first hermitage here in 1275. He came aged 40, shaken by an incident which caused him to review his way of life. Bent on seduction he chased a married woman through Palma on horseback; unable to shake him off, she lifted her blouse to reveal cancerous breasts. Llull retired in isolation to Puig de Randa to ponder a life of youthful excess. These days pilgrims to Puig de Randa are as likely to be weekend cyclists in search of a challenge as seekers after religious truth. The winding road to the summit leads to three separate hermitages. The lowest, Oratori de Nostra Senyora de Gràcia, is perched on a ledge in the cliff above a sheer 200-m drop. Further up is the Santuari de Sant Honorat and finally Santuari de Cura, where Llull lived. The sense of history is somewhat offset by the radio mast on the mountain top and the electric candles in the church, but this is still a special place. Visit the Sala Gramàtica to see Llull's original manuscripts and a bottle of 1934 Chartreuse made in the monastery, then look out from the terrace at the views of the plain, with Palma Bay and the isle of Cabrera in the distance. Simple rooms are available if you want to stay the night.

29D3
971 120260
Restaurant at Santuari de Cura (€€)
Free

Randa, the village at the foot of the mountain. The climb from here to the summit is one of Mallorca's most testing cycle rides

29F3
Snack bar (€)
From Palma to Cala Millor
Free
Cala Millor (➤ 48)

PUNTA DE N'AMER ✪

This 200-hectare nature reserve on a headland jutting out from the east coast is an oasis of peace amid a desert of high-rise apartments and hotels. Once, the whole coast was like this – thankfully, environmentalists have saved this small section from development. Walk south from Cala Millor, or north from Sa Coma, on a well-defined 1.5-km track. Eventually you reach the Castell de n'Amer, a 17th-century watchtower. Have a drink at the summit and look down at what you have left behind.

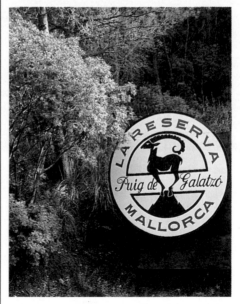

How to go walking in the mountains without getting lost – follow the easy waymarked trail around La Reserva

28B3
971 616622
Apr–Oct, daily 10–7; Nov–Mar, daily 10–6
Café (€)
Expensive
Galilea (➤ 56)

LA RESERVA ✪

On the slopes of Puig de Galatzó near the village of Puigpunyent, this nature reserve describes itself as 'Mallorca's paradise'. A 3-km trail of waymarked paths leads you through Mallorca's mountain scenery in less than two hours, past waterfalls and springs, olive trees and charcoal stoves. A series of boards provides background information on wildlife and mountain industries. Well laid out and interesting, the reserve gives you a feeling for the area. It will seem a bit sterile if you have been out in the mountains on your own – but it might help you to make sense of what you have already seen.

S'ALBUFERA   ✪✪

Just off the coast road 5km south of Port d'Alcúdia, the S'Albufera wetlands make a welcome relief from long stretches of crowded beach. Birdwatchers come from all over Europe to see rare migrants like Montagu's harriers and Eleanora's falcons; species breeding here include stonechats, moustached warblers and the long-eared owl. Ospreys leave their breeding sites on the cliffs to come here to fish; peregrines and hoopoes live here all year round.

The name derives from the Arabic for 'lagoon', but the site has been exploited since Roman times – Pliny writes of night herons, probably from S'Albufera, being sent to Rome as a gastronomic delicacy. The wetlands were drained for agriculture in the 19th century by a British company which subsequently went bankrupt; the network of canals dates from this time. Rice was introduced in the early 20th century, paper was manufactured from the reeds and sedge, and it is only since 1985, following fears that tourist development was damaging the area's fragile ecology, that S'Albufera has been a protected nature reserve. There are footpaths, cycle trails, birdwatching hides and an audio-visual display room where you can listen to birdsong.

🚼 29D4
✉ Carretera Port d'Alcúdia–Artà, km5
☎ 971 892250
🕐 Apr–Sep, daily 9–7; Oct–Mar, daily 9–5
🍴 Picnic area
🚌 From Port d'Alcúdia to Cala Rajada in summer
💷 Free
❓ Cars are not allowed in the reserve – leave them 1km from the visitor centre on the main road in the car park opposite Hotel Parc Natural

Get away from it all with a day at S'Albufera, walking among the marshes and listening to the birds

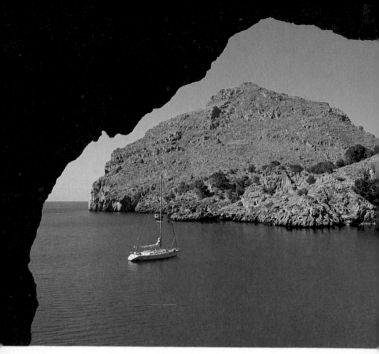

- 28C5
- Several restaurants (€–€€)
- From Port de Sóller (all year ☎ 971 630170)

SA CALOBRA ★★

Do not believe anyone who tells you that they have discovered the perfect unspoilt cove on the north coast – at least, not if its name is Sa Calobra. This is indeed a beautiful spot, which is why tour buses pour in by the dozen every day, even in winter.

The journey to Sa Calobra is as memorable as the bay itself. A twisting road around Puig Major plunges 800m in just 12km, turning 270 degrees at one point to loop under itself (a feature known as the 'Knotted Tie'). The easier approach is by boat from Port de Sóller, passing genuinely isolated bays with an excellent view of Puig Major, albeit spoilt by the military installations on the summit of Mallorca's highest mountain.

Once there, walk through 200m of tunnels to reach the Torrent de Pareis ('twin streams'), which begins several kilometres up in the mountains at the confluence of the torrents of Lluc and Gorg Blau. Up to 400m high and only 30m wide, with some sections never seeing daylight, this dramatic gorge culminates in a small pebble beach where you can picnic among the crowds. In summer, when the gorge is dry, you can hike inland between the cliffs; do not attempt this in winter.

A side turn off the road to Sa Calobra leads to Cala Tuent, a small cove with a sandy beach and a 13th-century church, Ermita de Sant Llorenç. Cala Tuent is likely to be quieter than Sa Calobra; but don't believe anyone who tells you they have discovered the *real* unspoilt cove...

View through a rock arch at Sa Calobra – Mallorca's most beautiful spot, or a place spoilt by tourists?

SA DRAGONERA ✪✪

This uninhabited island off Mallorca's western tip was the focus for a turning point in Mallorcan history in 1977, when it was occupied by environmentalists protesting against a planned tourist development. The campaigners won, the island became a nature reserve instead, the seabirds survived, and for the first time the authorities realised that mass tourism had reached its limit.

Six kilometres long and crowned by an ancient watchtower, Sa Dragonera takes its name from its shape, said to resemble a dragon. You can visit in summer by boat from Sant Elm; in winter you have to make do with views of the dragon from the beach at Sant Elm or from the climb to Sa Trapa (▶ below).

➕ 28A3
🚌 From Sant Elm (☎ 639 617545)
↔ Sant Elm (▶ below)

From Sant Elm you can climb to an abandoned monastery or take a boat to Sa Dragonera

SANT ELM ✪✪

The main reason for visiting Sant Elm, a laid-back resort with a fine sandy beach, is for the views of Sa Dragonera (▶ above). You can take a boat to the island from the jetty at the end of the main street, or sit outside the fish restaurants on the same jetty.

A challenging walk from Sant Elm leads to the abandoned Trappist monastery of Sa Trapa. Set out on Avinguda de la Trapa and climb through coastal *maquis* and pine, with fine views of Sa Dragonera. The round trip takes about three hours; a longer route is signposted beside the cemetery on the Sant Elm to Andratx road. Near here is the village of S'Arracó, built by Spanish settlers returning from the American colonies.

➕ 28A3
🍴 Choice of restaurants (€€)
🚌 From Andratx or Peguera
🚢 From Port d'Andratx and Peguera in summer
↔ Sa Dragonera (▶ above)

28C4
Local bars (€)
One or two buses daily from Palma
Market held Sat

Natura Parc
Carretera de Sineu, km15
971 144078
Apr–Oct, daily 10–7; Nov–Mar, daily 10–5
Expensive

28C4
Bars and cafés (€)
From Palma and Inca
Market held Sun

28B3
Bars and restaurants (€–€€)
From Palma
Rei en Jaume regatta in Jul

SANTA EUGÈNIA ✪
People argue over whether the mountains or the coast represent 'the real Mallorca', but the heart of the island is to be found in villages like this, surrounded by farmland with views to the sierra where the mountains rise out of the plain. The 6-km cart track to the neighbouring village of Sencelles offers good walking, and there is also the climb to Puig de Santa Eugènia (▶ 81). **Natura Parc**, on the edge of the village, is a popular family attraction with nature trails and indigenous farm animals as well as a butterfly garden.

SANTA MARIA DEL CAMÍ ✪
This market town on the Palma–Inca railway has developed a reputation as one of Mallorca's artistic centres. Most of the island's potters work close by, in Pòrtol (▶ 74), and Santa Maria is the centre of manufacture of *roba de llengues* ('cloth of tongues'), cotton woven into bright zigzag patterns and used in curtains, bedspreads and upholstery. Just off the main square is Ca'n Conrado, former Carmelite cloisters and a peaceful retreat from the traffic on the Palma road.

SANTA PONÇA ✪
Santa Ponça may look like just another beach resort but it has a permanent place in Mallorcan history. It was here that Jaume I landed in 1229 to begin his conquest of Mallorca, a conquest he described as 'the best thing man has done for a hundred years past'. A relief on a lárge cross above the marina, erected in 1929, records the event.

A Walk from Santa Eugènia

This simple walk gives spectacular views for the minimum of effort.

Leave the village of Santa Eugènia and head in the direction of Santa Maria del Camí. After 1km turn left along a narrow lane to Ses Coves.

The lane bends left, then descends, and you see Ses Coves ('the caves'), used at various times as pirate hideaways and wine cellars. One of them still contains an ancient winepress.

When the road divides, fork left; after five minutes you reach some iron gates at the entrance to a track on your right.

Here you have an optional detour to the summit of Puig d'En Marron, adding about an hour to your walk. Step over the low wall beside the iron gates, and climb until the road runs out. Continue along a mud track through the pine woods, keeping right at each fork, until you emerge onto a wide open plateau with wonderful views. Return to the iron gates by the same route and turn right to rejoin the main walk.

Follow the lane briefly uphill; when the lane divides, take the track on the left. After passing an arched entrance to a well, turn immediately left through an orchard towards a house. To the right of the house, the wall is marked with a red dot; climb from here to a pass.

Here you can clamber over a stone wall to your left to reach the cross on the summit of Puig de Santa Eugènia. This is the high point of the walk, with wonderful views that stretch across the plain to the mountains in the distance. On the opposite clifftop is one of Mallorca's oddest sights – the cockpit of a broken-up plane.

Retrace your steps to the stone wall and then follow the path that leads through the bushes on your left to return to Santa Eugènia.

Distance
4.5km (optional detour adds 3km)

Time
1–2 hours

Start/end point
Santa Eugènia
✚ 28C4
🚌 From Palma to Santa Maria del Camí with connecting bus to Santa Eugènia

Lunch
Ca Na Cantona (€)
✉ Carrer Balenguera, Santa Eugènia
☎ 971 144031

29E2

Bars and cafés (€)

From)

From Palma and Cala Figuera

Cala Figuera (➤ 47), Ses Salines (➤ 85)

Market held Wed, Sat; Sant Andreu *festa*, 30 Nov

SANTANYÍ ✪

Do not be surprised if the buildings in Santanyí look just that little bit more mellow than everywhere else – this small town is the source of the golden sandstone used in Palma's cathedral and La Llotja among others. The old gate, Sa Porta Murada, seen as you enter the town from Palma, is a good example of Santanyí stone and a reminder that this was once a walled town. The parish church of Sant Andreu Apòstel contains a massive rococo organ, designed by Jordi Bosch and brought here from a convent in Palma. The streets around the church are the focus for one of Mallorca's liveliest markets.

 29E3

Signposted from Felanitx–Porto Colom road

971 827282

Bar-restaurant (€) and picnic tables

Free

Felanitx (➤ 55)

SANTUARI DE SANT SALVADOR ✪✪

This old hermitage, 509m above sea level at the highest point of the Serra de Llevant, was the senior house of Mallorca's monastic order and the last to lose its monks, in 1992. It is still a popular place of pilgrimage, flanked by two enormous landmarks – to one side a 14-m stone cross, to the other a 35-m column topped by a statue of Christ holding out his right hand in blessing. The church contains a fine carved alabaster retable, but more interesting is the side chapel off the gatehouse, full of poignant mementos

The views from the Santuari de Sant Salvador stretch right across the central plain

and prayers to Our Lady. Like other former monasteries, Sant Salvador has a few simple rooms available for pilgrims.

The views from the terrace take in Cabrera, Cap de Formentor and several other hilltop sanctuaries dotted across the plain. From the statue of Christ you look out towards the Castell de Santueri, a 14th-century rock castle built into the cliffs on the site of a ruined Arab fortress.

SERRA DE TRAMUNTANA ✪✪✪

The 'mountains of the north wind' which run the length of Mallorca's north coast are home to the island's most spectacular landscapes. Pine-covered slopes almost lean into the sea; as you climb higher, forested hills give way to barren crags and peaks. The people of Mallorca have good reason to be grateful to the mountains. In winter they act as a buffer, shielding the plain from the fierce *tramuntana* wind and absorbing most of the island's rain and snow; in summer they provide a cool retreat from the heat of Palma and the south.

The Serra de Tramuntana runs for 88km from Andratx to Pollença, with the rocky outcrops of Sa Dragonera and Cap de Formentor at either end. Of the ten peaks over

✚ 28C4
↔ Lluc (➤ 23), Fornalutx (➤ 55), Sa Calobra (➤ 78), Sóller (➤ 86)
❓ Walking, birds, spring flowers

Fresh air, walking and sea views – the Serra de Tramuntana mountains (above) and Cap de Ses Salines (right)

1,000m, most are concentrated in the area around Lluc; the highest are Puig Major (1,445m) and Puig Massanella (1,349m). There are no rivers, though there are several mountain torrents which swell rapidly after rain – and the Cúber and Gorg Blau reservoirs, essential resources on an island so often affected by drought.

The mountains are best seen slowly, on foot; you smell the wild rosemary, hear the sheep-bells, frighten the goats, breathe in the air and marvel at pine trees growing out of red rock, a divine version of the colours of Mallorcan village houses. If you have to drive, take care – the roads here are the most dangerous on the island, and the endless procession of hairpin bends requires total concentration. The most dramatic drive of all is the C710 from Sóller to Lluc, traversing tunnels and gorges on its way between Puig Major and Puig Massanella.

SES COVETES ✪

The name of this village means 'small caves' and this is believed to refer to Roman burial chambers on the same site. Nowadays people come here for one thing – to get to Platja Es Trenc, a 3-km stretch of fine white sand backed by gentle dunes. This has long been an unofficial nudist beach, even during the puritanical Franco era. It no longer has the hippy atmosphere of old, but it still makes a peaceful, less commercial contrast to some of the other beaches on the south coast.

🗺 29D2
🚌 From Palma, Jul–Aug, 3 times a day

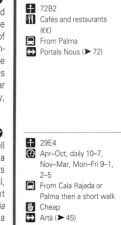

SES ILLETES ✪

This genteel resort, with its white villas and old-fashioned hotels, is for many people the most attractive in the whole Badia de Palma. Two small beaches look out over a pair of *illetes* (islets), the larger one crowned by an old watchtower. Its proximity to Palma means that you will never be alone here; in summer the buses from Palma to Ses Illetes are packed out at weekends. But if you want a base near the capital, combining a city break with a beach holiday, this could be just the place.

➕ 72B2
🍴 Cafés and restaurants (€€)
🚌 From Palma
↔ Portals Nous (▶ 72)

SES PAÏSSES ✪

Although not as extensive as the ruins at Capocorb Vell (▶ 50), this Bronze Age settlement near Artà is still a significant site and a link with Mallorcans of 3,000 years ago. Most impressive of all is the massive entrance portal, formed from three stone slabs weighing up to eight tonnes each. Inside there are several rooms and an *atalaia* (watchtower); the entire settlement is surrounded by a Cyclopean drystone wall.

➕ 29E4
🕐 Apr–Oct, daily 10–7, Nov–Mar, Mon–Fri 9–1, 2–5
🚌 From Cala Rajada or Palma then a short walk
💶 Cheap
↔ Artà (▶ 45)

SES SALINES ✪

This small town between Santanyí and Colònia de Sant Jordi is named after the nearby saltpans, which act as a magnet for migrant waders and wildfowl on their way from Africa to their breeding grounds in Europe each spring. Cap de Ses Salines, Mallorca's southernmost point, is another good spot for birdwatching. The town itself makes a pleasant place to stroll, with an abundance of local Santanyí sandstone which turns golden in the sun. Just outside Ses Salines, on the road to Santanyí, is **Botanicactus**, one of Europe's largest botanical gardens, with bamboo and palm trees and, extraordinarily diverse in form, dozens of varieties of cactus.

➕ 29D2
🍴 Bars and cafés (€)
🚌 Between Colònia de Sant Jordi and Santanyí
↔ Colònia de Sant Jordi (▶ 51), Santanyí (▶ 82)
❓ Market held Thu

Botanicactus
✉ Carretera Ses Salines–Santanyí, km1
☎ 971 649494
🕐 Jun–Sep, daily 9–7:30; Oct–May, daily 9–5
💶 Expensive

🏛 29D4
🍴 Several restaurants (€€)
🚌 From Palma
❓ Market held Wed

S'Estació
✉ Carrer Estació 2
☎ 971 520750
🕐 Mon–Fri 9:30–1:30, 4–7, Sat 9:30–1
🎫 Free

SINEU ✪✪✪

Sineu, at the geographical centre of Mallorca, comes alive each Wednesday morning at the island's most traditional market. It takes place on several levels. The sound of bleating leads you to the livestock market, where weather-beaten farmers haggle over the price of sheep before heading for the town's *celler* restaurants for an early brunch. Further up, on the way to the church, you pass the symbol of Sineu, a winged lion; near here are numerous stalls selling leather, lace and pearls. Eventually you reach Sa Plaça, the church square, where the action is liveliest of all, as local housewives turn out to buy the week's food. Buckets of olives, strings of tomatoes, bags of squirming snails – they are all here, along with plenty of fresh fruit, vegetables and flowers. Get to Sineu early, before the tour buses arrive, to catch the flavour of a traditional country market. Good buys include dried figs and apricots, pottery from Pòrtol and baskets from Sudan. Also in Sineu is **S'Estació**, an unusual modern art gallery based in the old station.

The winged lion, honouring St Mark, is the symbol of Sineu

🏛 28C4
🍴 Wide choice of bars and restaurants (€–€€)
🚌 From Palma; tram to Port de Sóller
↔ Fornalutx (▶ 55), Port de Sóller (▶ 70)
❓ Market held Sat; *Moros i Cristians*, re-enactment of a 1561 battle in which local women helped to defeat a band of Turkish pirates, 8–10 May

SÓLLER ✪✪✪

Set in a lush valley of orange groves between the mountains and the sea, Sóller is popular with day trippers who arrive on the vintage train from Palma (▶ 71) and seem to do little but sit outside the cafés in Plaça Constitució soaking up the atmosphere and the sun. With several *tapas* bars, a fine selection of pastry shops, local ice cream and freshly squeezed orange juice, there is little temptation to move on.

Sóller grew rich on oranges and the results can be seen in its extravagant *modernista* architecture. The church of Sant Bartomeu has a 1912 arched tower suspended above the rose window, with spires like huge needles pointing into the air. The same architect, Gaudí's pupil Joan Rubió, designed the Banco Central Hispano next door.

A stroll to the cemetery above the station, flanked by cypress trees and filled with potted plants, gives a clue to Sóller's history. Several of the epitaphs are in French, revealing the significant French community of the town, descendants of those who came to make their fortune by exporting oranges.

Sóller has two museums worth visiting. The **Natural Science Museum**, in a turn-of-the-19th-century manor house on the Palma road, has a collection of fossils and a botanical garden. The **Museu de Sóller** is an 18th-century town house in the town centre, filled with antiques and relics of old Sóller.

A final word of advice: come here by train, rather than car. The climb over the Coll de Sóller, with its 57 hairpin bends, is the most terrifying drive in Mallorca. There is now a controversial new road tunnel through the mountain, but the train journey from Palma is a delight so why not give yourself a treat.

Sóller's main square (above) contains some interesting modern architecture, such as the bank designed by Joan Rubió (left)

Natural Science Museum
- ✉ Carretera Palma–Port de Sóller
- ☎ 971 634014
- 🕐 Tue–Sat 10–6, Sun 10–2
- 💵 Cheap

Museu de Sóller
- ✉ Carrer de Sa Mar 9
- ☎ 971 634663
- 🕐 Mon–Fri 11–4, Sat 11–1:30
- 💵 Donation

🏠 28B4
📮 Carretera Valldemossa–
Deià
📞 971 639158
🕐 Apr–Sep, Mon–Sat
9:30–2, 3–7; Oct–Mar,
Mon–Sat 10–2, 3–5:30
🍴 Mirador de Na Foradada
(€€)
🚌 From Palma,
Valldemossa and Port de
Sóller
💷 Cheap
🔁 Deià (▶ 22)

SON MARROIG ✪✪

Of all the famous foreigners attracted to Mallorca's
northwest coast, none is so admired locally as 'S'Arxiduc',
Archduke Ludwig Salvator. Born in 1847 in the Pitti Palace,
Florence, the son of Leopold III of Tuscany and Marie
Antoinette de Bourbon, he came to Mallorca 20 years later
to escape from Viennese court life and immediately fell in
love with the island. An ecologist before it was
fashionable, and an early hippy who wore Mallorcan
peasant clothes, he bought up estates along the coast in
an effort to save them from development, and devoted
himself to studying and recording Mallorcan wildlife and
traditions. His seven-volume *Las Baleares* took 20 years to
produce and is still an
authority on its subject. He
died in 1915 in a Bohemian
castle.

The Archduke's home at
Son Marroig, outside Deià,
has been turned into a shrine
to his memory, with his
photographs, paintings and
books and a museum
devoted to his life. In the
gardens is a white marble
rotunda, made from Carrara
marble and imported from
Italy, where you can sit and
gaze at the Na Foradada
('pierced rock') peninsula,
jutting out to sea with a
gaping 18-m hole at its
centre. Ask at the house for
permission to walk onto the
peninsula.

*Private view – the
Archduke's garden looks
down over the peninsula
of Na Foradada*

Did you know ?

*Another of the Archduke's estates, Miramar, was founded
as a hermitage by Ramón Llull (▶ 14) in 1276. It has
recently opened to the public – you can visit the library,
see the collection of old maps and stroll around the
gardens admiring the sea views. It is found close to Son
Marroig on the road to Valldemossa.*

VALLDEMOSSA (▶ 26, TOP TEN)

The Archduke's Bridlepath

This walk was mapped out by Archduke Ludwig Salvator during tours of his estates by mule; as well as spectacular coastal views, it gives an introduction to traditional mountain industries. You pass *sitjas* (round charcoal ovens), *casas de neu* (snow pits where winter snows were stored beneath a layer of ash), *forns de calç* (lime kilns) and *caças a coll* (thrush nets slung between the trees). The route is for experienced walkers only. Take food and water, a map, compass and whistle, and protection from sun, wind and rain. The weather on the mountains can change very quickly.

Distance
13km

Time
6 hours

Start/end point
Valldemossa

 28B4
From Palma, Deià or Port de Sóller

Lunch
Take a picnic

Begin at the car park opposite Bar Sa Mata on the main road through Valldemossa. Climb the hill behind the car park, towards the cemetery. Take the second right (Carrer Joan Fuster), then first left (Carrer de les Oliveres), continuing onto a rough track when the road runs out.

You climb gently at first, towards a group of pines, then more steeply, following red waymarks to a clearing. From here it is a short, tough climb to a mirador and the start of the Camí de S'Arxiduc, marked by a ruined stone refuge.

Follow the waymarks onto a high plateau and continue for about two hours.

For the best views of all, a one-hour diversion (just as the main path bears round to the right to begin its descent) takes you to the summit of the Teix, from where most of Mallorca is visible on a clear day.

The path drops back down to Valldemossa through a wooded valley, passing a shelter where you can camp in summer.

For a shorter walk to the foot of the Teix, you can simply do the final section in reverse. Leave Valldemossa by climbing past Son Gual, the large old house with a tower, seen just above the main road on the right as you enter from Palma. Turn left after 10 minutes onto a wide track signposted 'Refugi'. The climb through the valley to the shelter and back will take a couple of hours if you walk briskly.

+ 29D3
From Palma and Manacor
? Market held Wed

Els Calderers
Carretera Palma–
Manacor, km37
971 526069
Apr–Sep, daily 10–6;
Oct–Mar, daily 10–5
Café (€)
Expensive

*Vilafranca is famed for its
melons and sun-dried
tomatoes*

VILAFRANCA DE BONANY ✪

As you drive through this small town on the old road from Palma to Manacor, you cannot help noticing the strings of vegetables hanging outside several of the shops – peppers, aubergines, garlic and, above all, tomatoes. These are the famous *tomàtigues de ramallet*, sold on their stalks to be spread over *pa amb oli*. Vilafranca is also known for its honeydew melons, whose harvest is celebrated with a large melon festival each September. The other reason for coming here, apart from food, is to visit **Els Calderers**, a manor house between Vilafranca and Sant Joan. This was once at the centre of a great wine estate but like so many others it fell victim to the phylloxera disease. Reopened in 1993, the 18th-century house is now a museum of Mallorcan furniture and traditions; you can visit the wine cellar, granary, bakery, chapel and wash-house as well as wander around the main house with its paintings, guns and hunting trophies.

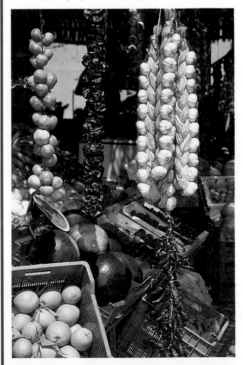

Where To...

Above: *Floorshow at
Casino Mallorca*;
Right: *Wall
plaque in Palma*

Palma

Prices
Prices are approximate, based on a three-course meal for one without drinks and service:

€ = under €15
€€ = €15–30
€€€= over €30

Most restaurants serve a *menú del día* at lunchtime (▶ 96) which will usually work out much cheaper. It is normal practice to add about 10 per cent to the bill as a tip.

A Warning
Opening hours change frequently, and many restaurants take an annual holiday in winter. It is always a good idea to telephone before setting out.

Afrikana (€€)
Spicy African cooking served with honey and hibiscus wine in this friendly restaurant near Santa Catalina market.
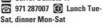 Carrer Dameto 17
☎ 971 287007 🕐 Lunch Tue-Sat, dinner Mon-Sat

Aramis (€€€)
Modern Mediterranean cuisine and a good-value set menu in a town house behind La Llotja.
✉ Carrer Montenegro 1
☎ 971 725232 🕐 Lunch Mon–Fri, dinner Mon–Sat

Baisakhi (€€)
High-class Indian cuisine; no choice, just an excellent daily set menu.
✉ Passeig Marítim 8
☎ 971 736806 🕐 Dinner Tue–Sat

La Bodeguilla (€€)
Modern variations of classic Spanish cuisine; the same owners have a stylish *tapas* bar next door.
✉ Carrer Sant Jaume 1 and 3
☎ 971 718274 🕐 Mon–Sat 1–11:30

Bon Lloc (€)
Vegetarian restaurant with good-value four-course set lunch.
✉ Carrer Sant Feliu 7 ☎ 971 718617 🕐 Lunch Mon–Sat

Caballito de Mar (€€)
Popular fish restaurant on the seafront.
✉ Passeig Sagrera 5
☎ 971 721074 🕐 Lunch, dinner. Closed Mon

Ca'n Carlos (€€)
One of the few restaurants in central Palma to focus on traditional Mallorcan cuisine.
✉ Carrer de l'Aigua 5 ☎ 971 713869 🕐 Lunch, dinner. Closed Sun

Candela (€€€)
In a street better known for its *tapas* bars, this place offers fresh fish and creative Mediterranean cuisine.
✉ Carrer dels Apuntadors 14
☎ 971 724428 🕐 Dinner. Closed Wed

Ca'n Eduardo (€€)
Traditional fish restaurant above the fish market.
✉ Es Moll de Pescadors
☎ 971 721182 🕐 Lunch, dinner. Closed Sun

Ca'n Joan de S'Aigo (€)
Classy café where Joan Miró used to go for hot chocolate, almond ice cream and *ensaimadas*.
✉ Carrer Sant Sanç 10; Barò Santa Maria del Sepulcre 5
☎ 971 710759 🕐 Closed Tue

Celler Sa Premsa (€€)
Mallorcan classics in a converted garage lined with wine vats and faded bullfighting posters.
✉ Plaça Bisbe Berenguer de Palou 8 ☎ 971 723529
🕐 Lunch, dinner. Closed Sun

Chopin (€€€)
Top-notch Swiss-Mediterranean dishes on a garden terrace in the back streets close to the Born.
✉ Carrer Ca'n Puigdorfila 2
☎ 971 723556 🕐 Lunch Mon–Fri, dinner Mon–Sat

Fábrica 23 (€)
One of the hottest restaurants in town is run by an English chef in the buzzing Santa Catalina district. Go early if you want a table at lunchtime.

✉ **Carrer Fábrica 23**
☎ 971 453125 🕙 Lunch, dinner, Tue–Sat

Flor de Loto (€€)
Intimate bistro offering vegetarian and fish dishes in the back streets around La Llotja. Flamenco guitarist at weekends.
✉ **Carrer Vallseca 7**
☎ 971 717778 🕙 Dinner. Closed Mon

Fundació la Caixa (€€)
Cocktails, cakes, sandwiches and serious meals in the bar of the former Gran Hotel.
✉ **Plaça Weyler 3**
☎ 971 728077 🕙 Lunch, dinner. Closed Sun dinner

Koldo Royo (€€€)
High-class Basque and Mallorcan nouvelle cuisine on the waterfront, with windows overlooking the bay.
✉ **Passeig Marítim 3**
☎ 971 732435 🕙 Lunch Tue–Sun, dinner Tue–Sat

La Lubina (€€)
A fish restaurant on the quay – try *lubina en sal*, sea bass baked in rock salt.
✉ **Es Moll Vell** ☎ 971 723350
🕙 Lunch, dinner daily

Na Bauçana (€)
Friendly vegetarian restaurant with set-price midweek lunch.
✉ **Carrer Santa Bàrbara 4**
☎ 971 721886 🕙 Lunch Mon–Fri

Opio (€€)
Funky 'Mediterrasian' fusion food at an ethnic-style boutique hotel.
✉ **Carrer Montenegro 12**
☎ 971 425450 🕙 Lunch, dinner. Closed Mon

El Pilon (€€)
Good little *tapas* bar in an alley off the Born. A good lively setting with lots of atmosphere.
✉ **Carrer Ca'n Cifre 3**
☎ 971 717590 🕙 Lunch, dinner. Closed Sun

Sa Llimona (€)
Create your own *pa amb oli* with a huge choice of toppings – ham, salami, anchovies, cheese. Good salads too.
✉ **Carrer Fábrica 27A** ☎ 971 736096 🕙 Dinner daily

Sa Volta (€)
Authentic cellar bar with hams hanging from the ceiling – one of numerous *tapas* bars along the same street.
✉ **Carrer dels Apuntadors 5**
🕙 Lunch, dinner Mon–Sat

Taberna de la Bóveda (€€)
Great *tapas* on a terrace facing the harbour. The original La Bóveda is just around the corner at Carrer Boteria 3. Roasted mushrooms; red peppers and much more.
✉ **Passeig Sagrera 3** ☎ 971 720026 🕙 Lunch, dinner Mon–Sat

Taberna del Caracol (€€)
Great little *tapas* restaurant in an old stone house close to the Arab Baths.
✉ **Carrer Sant Alonso 2**
☎ 971 714908 🕙 Lunch, dinner. Closed Sun

Txakoli (€€)
Charcoal-grilled meat is the speciality at this busy Basque joint in the heart of Santa Catalina.
✉ **Carrer Fábrica 14** ☎ 971 282126 🕙 Lunch Mon–Fri, dinner Mon–Sat

Tapas

Tapas are a Spanish institution. Originally a free 'lid' (*tapa*) of ham across a drink, nowadays they consist of small portions of everything from octopus to olives. Locals eat *tapas* before going out to eat, but several portions can make an unusual meal in itself. The best place to eat *tapas* in Mallorca is in the area around La Llotja in Palma.

Around the Island

Eating Out in Mallorca
The Spanish like to eat late – many restaurants do not even open until 1:30 at lunchtime and 8:30 in the evening, and fill up an hour or two later. It is a good idea to book a table in advance, especially in summer and at weekends. Formal dress is rarely necessary – even at the best establishments smart casual is the rule. And children are always welcome!

Alcúdia
Ca'n Simó (€)
Stylish vegetarian cooking in a chic townhouse hotel. The four-course lunch menu is excellent value.
✉ Carrer d'en Serra 22
☎ 971 542673 🕐 Lunch, dinner. Closed Mon

Khum Phanit's S'Aufabi (€)
Old town branch of well-known Thai restaurant, offering spring rolls, spicy snacks and one-plate meals with rice or noodles.
✉ Carrer d'en Serra 5
☎ 971 547760 🕐 Lunch, dinner. Closed Mon

Sa Plaça (€€)
Traditional and modern Spanish and Mediterranean cuisine – how about courgettes stuffed with pine nuts, raisins, black pudding and Mallorcan cheese?
✉ Plaça Constitució 1 ☎ 971 542678 🕐 Thu-Tue 12-12

Algaida
Cal Dimoni (€€)
Meat and blood sausages grilled over an open fire at the 'house of the devil'.
✉ Carretera Palma–Manacor, km21 ☎ 971 665035
🕐 Noon–midnight. Closed Wed

Ca'n Mateu (€€)
Roast suckling pig and other specialities beside a pool and children's play area.
✉ Carretera Palma–Manacor, km21 ☎ 971 665036
🕐 Lunch, dinner. Closed Tue

Es 4 Vents (€€)
Mallorcan and Spanish classics, very popular for Sunday lunch.
✉ Carretera Palma–Manacor, km21 ☎ 971 665173
🕐 Lunch, dinner. Closed Thu

Hostal d'Algaida (€€)
Mallorcan cuisine in an old coaching inn – try croquettes of spinach with monkfish.
✉ Carretera Palma–Manacor, km21 ☎ 971 665109
🕐 Lunch, dinner daily

Artà
Café Parisien (€€)
Coffee, pastries, salads and Mediterranean cuisine in an arty café on the main street.
✉ Carrer Ciutat 18
☎ 971 835440 🕐 Lunch, dinner daily

Binissalem
Scott's Bistro (€€)
Cosy, candlelit ambience and a menu of freshly prepared market cuisine – steaks, fish, vegetables. A good place for a romantic meal.
✉ Carrer Pou Bo 20 ☎ 971 870076 🕐 Mon-Sat 7PM-midnight

Cala Rajada
Ses Rotges (€€€)
Quality French cooking with prices to match at one of Mallorca's top hotels.
✉ Carrer Rafael Blanes 21
☎ 971 563108 🕐 Lunch, dinner daily. Closed Nov–Mar

Cala de Sant Vicenç
Cavall Bernat (€€€)
Top-notch Mallorcan meat and fish dishes, such as spiced turbot and roast suckling lamb.
✉ Carrer Maressers 2
☎ 971 530250 🕐 Dinner daily

Meson Ca'n Torrat (€€)
Mallorcan classics like *llom amb col* and roast shoulder of lamb in a rustic bar opposite the church.
✉ Carrer Major 29 ☎ 971 670682 🕐 Lunch, dinner. Closed Thu

Capdepera

Café de l'Orient (€)
Lively *tapas* bar on the market square.
✉ Plaça de l'Orient 4
☎ 971 563098 🕐 Daily 8AM–midnight

Castell d'Alaró

Es Verger (€€)
Roast lamb is cooked in a wood-fired oven at this farmhouse restaurant halfway up to the castle.
✉ On the way to Castell d'Alaró ☎ 971 182126
🕐 Lunch, dinner daily

Colònia de Sant Jordi

Marisol (€€)
A good old-fashioned family beach terrace right on the harbour, offering fresh fish, paella, pizza and pasta dishes.
✉ On the harbourside ☎ 971 655070 🕐 Mar-Oct, lunch, dinner daily

Deià

El Olivo (€€€)
Fine *nouvelle cuisine* in a romantic setting – one of the best restaurants on the island for a special occasion. There is even a vegetarian gourmet tasting menu.
✉ La Residencia hotel
☎ 971 639392 🕐 Lunch, dinner daily

Es Racó d'es Teix (€€€)
Creative Mediterranean cooking in an old stone house with a delightful shady terrace.
✉ Carrer Vinya Vella 6
☎ 971 639501 🕐 Lunch, dinner. Closed Tue

Jaume (€€)
A Deià institution, offering Mallorcan dishes like *tumbet* and *frit mallorquí* in defiance of the trend towards new

Mediterranean cuisine.
✉ Carrer Arxiduc Lluis Salvador 24 ☎ 971 639029
🕐 Lunch, dinner. Closed Mon

Mirador de Na Foradada (€€)
Dine with a view of the northwest coast. Typical Mallorcan/Spanish cuisine.
✉ Son Marroig, Carretera Valldemossa–Deià
☎ 971 639026 🕐 Lunch, dinner. Closed Thu

Sebastian (€€€)
Modern Mediterranean cooking with an emphasis on fresh fish in an old town house with bare stone walls.
✉ Carrer Felipe Bauza
☎ 971 639417 🕐 Dinner. Closed Wed and Nov–Mar

Fornalutx

Ca'n Antuna (€€)
Mallorcan cuisine on a shady terrace with views of orange groves and distant peaks.
✉ Carrer Arbona Colom 7
☎ 971 633068 🕐 Lunch, dinner. Closed Mon

Gènova

Meson Ca'n Pedro (€€)
The busiest restaurant in Mallorca turns out huge portions of barbecued meat at generous prices in a village on the outskirts of Palma.
✉ Carrer Rector Vives
☎ 971 702162 🕐 Lunch, dinner. Closed Tue

Inca

Celler Ca'n Amer (€€)
This busy *celler* beside the covered market was chosen to represent Balearic cooking at the Expo 92 fair in Seville.
✉ Carrer Pau 39 ☎ 971 501261 🕐 Lunch, dinner. Closed Sun

Cellers
A *celler* is an old wine-cellar converted into a restaurant specialising in traditional Mallorcan cuisine. Real basement *cellers* have wine vats to prove it, but nowadays the term is used for any old-style restaurant. *Cellers* are good places to go in order to try Mallorcan classics like *llom amb col* (pork wrapped in cabbage) or *frit mallorquí* (fried offal). The best *cellers* are found in market towns like Inca and Sineu.

Menú del Día
Most restaurants offer a *menú del día* at lunchtime – a set-price three-course meal with water or wine included. You won't get much choice (typically soup or salad, meat or fish and fruit or ice cream) but the food will be freshly cooked, filling and sometimes surprisingly good. A three-course lunch in a small rural town will often cost less than a single portion of *tapas* in Palma.

Celler Ca'n Ripoli (€€)
Founded in 1782 with dark wooden beams, chandeliers and wine vats around the walls. Mallorcan cuisine.
✉ Carrer Jaume Armengol 4 ☎ 971 500024 🕐 Lunch, dinner. Closed Sun

Celler Son Aloy (€€)
Rustic grill and wine-tasting cellar in the middle of Mallorca's biggest vineyard, just outside Inca.
✉ Carretera Inca-Sencelles km3 ☎ 971 502302 🕐 Lunch Tue-Sun, dinner Wed-Sat

Jardines d'Alfábia
Ses Porxeres (€€)
Catalan game dishes in a barn beside the Alfábia gardens.
✉ Carretera Palma–Sóller ☎ 971 613762 🕐 Lunch, dinner. Closed Sun dinner, Mon

Montuïri
Puig de Sant Miquel (€€)
Roast kid and other Mallorcan classics served on a terrace beside a hilltop hermitage.
✉ Carretera de Manacor, km31 ☎ 971 646314 🕐 Lunch, dinner daily

Orient
Dalt Muntanya (€€)
Pa amb oli at lunchtime and modern Mallorcan cooking in the evening on the terrace of this newly renovated hotel.
✉ Carretera de Bunyola ☎ 971 615373 🕐 Lunch, dinner daily

L'Hermitage (€€€)
Choose between a flower-filled terrace or a dining room full of antiques at this 17th-century manor house and hotel. The menu is based on fresh local ingredients.
✉ Carretera Alaró–Bunyola ☎ 971 180303 🕐 Lunch, dinner daily

Mandala (€€)
Innovative French–Indian cuisine by a couple from Geneva, in a house at the very top of the village.
✉ Carrer Nou 1 ☎ 971 615285 🕐 Jun–Aug, dinner Mon–Sat; Sep–May, lunch Tue–Sun, dinner Fri–Sat

Restaurant Orient (€)
Roast lamb, snails and other rustic Mallorcan dishes in a popular village bar.
✉ Carretera de Bunyola ☎ 971 615153 🕐 Lunch, dinner. Closed Sun dinner, Tue

Palma Nova
Ciro's (€€)
Pizzas and other Italian/Mediterranean specialities served on a terrace overlooking the beach.
✉ Passeig del Mar 3 ☎ 971 681052 🕐 Lunch, dinner daily

Peguera
La Gran Tortuga (€€)
Seafood and European cuisine is served on a terrace overlooking a pretty bay – you can order your meal then take a dip in the swimming pool while it is being cooked.
✉ Aldea Cala Fornells 1 ☎ 971 686023 🕐 Lunch, dinner. Closed Mon

Petra
Es Celler (€€)
Typical Mallorcan *celler* bar with an olive press and hearty peasant cooking.
✉ Carrer de l'Hospital 46 ☎ 971 561056 🕐 Lunch, dinner. Closed Mon

Sa Plaça (€€)
Prawns with chocolate sauce is just one of the old-style Mallorcan dishes at this small hotel-restaurant on the main square.

✉ Plaça Ramón Llull 4
☎ 971 561646 🕐 Lunch,
dinner. Closed Tue

Pollença

Balaixa (€€)
Dine on the terrace in
summer or indoors in winter
at this old Mallorcan
farmhouse with a private
pool on the main road to Port
de Pollença.
✉ Carretera Port de Pollença
☎ 971 530659 🕐 Lunch,
dinner daily

Cantonet (€€)
Italian restaurant featuring
salads, fresh pasta and
vegetarian dishes.
✉ Carrer Montesió 20
☎ 971 530429 🕐 Dinner.
Closed Tue

Clivia (€€)
This popular restaurant is in
an old manor house. Try the
local speciality, roasted sea
bass.
✉ Avinguda Pollentia 9
☎ 971 533635 🕐 Lunch,
dinner. Closed Wed

La Font del Gall (€€)
French style in an intimate
back-street restaurant close
to the 'cockerel fountain'
from which it takes its
unusual name.
✉ Carrer Montesió 4 ☎ 971
530396 🕐 Apr–Oct, dinner
daily,

Porreres

Centro (€)
Cheap and cheerful – Spanish
classics served in an old
theatre and church hall. If you
can try to get a table on the
small patio garden in
summer.
✉ Avinguda Bisbe Campins 13
☎ 971 168372 🕐 Lunch,
dinner. Closed Sun dinner

Port d'Alcúdia

Bogavante (€€€)
The rice and fresh fish
dishes are especially good at
this seafood restaurant
facing the harbour.
✉ Carrer Teodor Canet 2
☎ 971 547364 🕐 Lunch,
dinner. Closed Mon

Khum Phanit's (€)
This is a real surprise –
authentic Thai cooking and
the bonus of extremely good
value.
✉ Avinguda de la Platja 7
☎ 971 548141 🕐 Lunch,
dinner. Closed Mon

Port d'Andratx

Miramar (€€€)
Lobster and seafood beside
the harbour. You need to
take out a mortgage before
eating here.
✉ Avinguda Mateo Bosch 22
☎ 971 671617 🕐 Feb–Sep,
lunch, dinner daily

Rocamar (€€)
This is the place to try Galician
and Mallorcan seafood
specialities in a perfect setting
at the end of the promenade.
✉ Carrer d'Almirante Riera
Alemany 29 ☎ 971 671261
🕐 Lunch, dinner daily

Port de Pollença

Ca'n Cuarassa (€€)
Top-notch Mediterranean
cuisine in a delightful setting
with views across the bay.
✉ Carretera Port de Pollença-
Alcúdia ☎ 971 864266
🕐 Lunch, dinner daily

Juma (€)
A great selection of *tapas*
served throughout the day at
this old-style hotel on the
main square.
✉ Plaça Major 9 ☎ 971
533258 🕐 Daily 8AM-midnight

Fish and Seafood
Mallorca's fish stocks have
long been in decline and
most of the fish on sale on
the island is imported from
mainland Spain and
beyond. By law, restaurant
menus should state
whether fish is fresh or
frozen – prices for frozen
fish are invariably cheaper.
Fresh fish is always
excellent; specialities
include lobster casserole,
sea bass in rock salt and
greixonera de peix, a
hearty fish stew cooked in
an earthenware bowl.

Olives

Olives were introduced to Mallorca by the Romans and have been used ever since – the oil for cooking and soap, the branches for firewood, the wood for carving into bowls and spoons. Almost every meal begins with bread and olives, for which you may pay a small charge. Bread and olives are also at the heart of *pa amb oli*, the favourite Mallorcan snack – bread rubbed with tomato, drizzled with olive oil and topped with ham or cheese.

Siurell (€€

Grilled meat is the speciality at this waterfront restaurant, in a tourist area at the southern end of the beach.

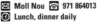 **Carrer Cirerer** ☎ **971 865427** 🕐 **Lunch, dinner daily in summer**

Stay (€€€)

This is a popular fish restaurant on the jetty – try the *parrillada*, a fish and seafood mixed grill.

Moll Nou ☎ **971 864013** 🕐 **Lunch, dinner daily**

Port de Sóller

Celler d'es Port (€€)

Enormous helpings of Mallorcan classics like roast shoulder of lamb with oregano.

Carrer Antoni Montis 17 ☎ **971 630654** 🕐 **Lunch Thu–Tue, dinner Sat**

Es Faro (€€€)

Fresh fish in a magnificent setting, high above the fishing port overlooking the sea.

Cap Gros de Maleta ☎ **971 633752** 🕐 **Lunch, dinner. Closed Tue in winter**

Portals Nous

Tahini (€€€)

There are numerous swanky bistros around the marina at Puerto Portals but this one stands out for its minimalist design and Japanese-inspired fusion food.

Puerto Portals ☎ **971 676025** 🕐 **Lunch, dinner. Closed Mon**

Porto Colom

Celler Sa Sinia (€€)

Seafood specialities in a perfect waterfront spot.

Carrer des Pescadors 25 ☎ **971 824323** 🕐 **Lunch, dinner. Closed Mon**

Colón (€€€)

One of the top restaurants on the island, beside the sea, with a terrace overlooking the fishing port. Modern Mediterranean cuisine.

Carrer Cristobal Colón 7 ☎ **971 824783** 🕐 **Lunch, dinner. Closed Wed**

Randa

Celler Bar Randa (€)

Good-value Mallorcan cuisine in the village bar beside the church.

Carrer Església 20 ☎ **971 660989** 🕐 **Lunch, dinner. Closed Wed**

Es Reco de Randa (€€)

Mallorcan and Spanish cooking in an old hotel at the foot of Puig de Randa.

Carrer Font 21 ☎ **971 660997** 🕐 **Lunch, dinner daily**

S'Arracó

La Tulipe (€€)

Modern European cooking in a New Age arty atmosphere.

Plaça de Toledo 2 ☎ **971 671449** 🕐 **Dinner Mon–Sat**

Santa Eugènia

L'Escargot (€€)

French classics and a menu that changes regularly according to what is in the market. Also pancakes, cheeses and French and Spanish *tapas*.

Carrer Major 48 ☎ **971 144535** 🕐 **Dinner Wed–Sat, Sun lunch**

Santa Maria del Camí

Ca'n Calet (€€)

Bustling restaurant just off the main road in an old townhouse with stone arches and a pretty garden. Good value Spanish/Mallorcan food.

📭 Plaça dels Hostals 26
☎ 971 620173 🕐 Lunch, dinner daily

Moli d'es Torrent (€€€)
German chef Peter Himbert offers a personal interpretation of German and Mallorcan cuisine at this restaurant in an old windmill.
📭 Carretera Bunyola 75
☎ 971 140503 🕐 Lunch, dinner. Closed Thu

Read's (€€€)
British chef Marc Fosh conjures up sublime creations such as grilled sea-bass in liquorice sauce at this grand country hotel. The atmosphere is eccentric and the décor is over-the-top but this is one of the top culinary experiences on Mallorca.
📭 Carretera Santa Maria-Alaró ☎ 971 140261
🕐 Lunch, dinner daily

Simply Fosh (€€)
If you don't want to splash out, Fosh offers simpler bistro fare, such as risottos, curries and fish soup, at more affordable prices.
📭 Carretera Santa Maria-Alaró ☎ 971 140261
🕐 Lunch, dinner daily

Sant Elm
El Pescador (€€)
Fish restaurant on the jetty with its own fishing boat and fine views of Sa Dragonera.
📭 Avinguda Jaume 1 ☎ 971 239198 🕐 Lunch, dinner daily

Sineu
Celler Sa Font (€€)
Traditional *celler* with wine vats lining the walls – very busy on market day (Wed).
📭 Plaça d'Espanya 18
☎ 971 520313 🕐 Lunch, dinner daily

Sóller
Bens d'Avall (€€€)
Creative Mediterranean cuisine in a fabulous setting on a terrace overlooking Mallorca's northwest coast.
📭 Carretera Deià–Sóller, Urbanización Costa de Deià
☎ 971 632381 🕐 Lunch, Tue–Sun, dinner Tue–Sat (Apr–Nov)

Café Sóller (€)
Buzzy café and art gallery on the main square offering fresh pasta, salads, *tapas* and cakes.
📭 Plaça Constitució ☎ 971 630010 🕐 Lunch daily, dinner Sun-Fri

Ca N'Ai (€€€)
Fine food and elegant service on the terrace of a country house hotel surrounded by orange groves.
📭 Camí Son Sales
☎ 971 632494 🕐 Feb–Oct, lunch, dinner. Closed Mon

Sa Cova (€€)
Mallorcan classics (stuffed aubergines and rabbit with garlic) in a great position.
📭 Plaça Constitució 7
☎ 971 633222 🕐 Lunch, dinner. Closed Sun dinner and Mon

Valldemossa
Ca'n Costa (€€)
Mallorcan and Spanish cuisine in a converted oil mill.
📭 Carretera Valldemossa–Deià, km2.5 ☎ 971 612263
🕐 Lunch, dinner. Closed Tue

Valldemossa (€€€)
Fine wine, food and service in a luxury hotel with a terrace overlooking the village.
📭 Carretera Vieja de Valldemossa ☎ 971 612626
🕐 Lunch, dinner daily

Coffee and Liqueurs
In Spain, *un café* after the meal means only one thing: *café solo*, served short, strong and black, with sugar. Ask for a *carajillo* and it will have brandy added, or a bottle of *coñac* left on the table for you to help yourself. If the waiter brings a liqueur with your coffee, this is a *copa*, a treat on the house. Enjoy!

Palma

Prices
Prices are for a double room, excluding breakfast and VAT:

€ = under €60
€€ = €60–120
€€€= over €120

These prices will be much lower if you book as part of a package holiday. Most hotels in the main resorts are block-booked by tour operators and it is through them that you will get the cheapest deals.

What Does It Mean?
All accommodation in Spain is strictly classified and graded by the government. Hotels are graded from one to five stars; *hostals*, with fewer facilities but often just as comfortable, from one star to three. A *hotel residencia* or *hostal residencia* is one that does not serve evening meals.

Born (€€)
Two-star *hotel residencia* in a converted mansion near the Born. The best value if you want character in the old city.
✉ **Carrer Sant Jaume 3**
☎ **971 712942; www.hotel born.com** 🕐 **All year**

Ciutat Jardí (€€€)
One of Mallorca's earliest tourist hotels has reopened after a major renovation. The Moorish-style building is behind the beach, with fabulous views of Palma, a 1-hour walk around the bay.
✉ **Carrer Illa de Malta 14, Ciutat Jardí** ☎ **971 260007; www.hciutatj.com** 🕐 **All year**

Cuba (€)
Friendly budget hostel with clean, comfortable rooms. In a Modernist building in the trendy Santa Catalina district.
✉ **Carrer Sant Magí 1** ☎ **971 738159** 🕐 **All year**

Dalt Muranda (€€)
Just eight elegant rooms furnished with antiques in a restored Gothic manor house near the cathedral.
✉ **Carrer Almudaina 6A**
☎ **971 425300; www.hotel daltmurada.com** 🕐 **All year**

Meliá Victoria (€€€)
A huge modern hotel that dominates the harbour area. Most rooms have views of the cathedral and bay.
✉ **Avinguda Joan Miró 21**
☎ **971 732542; www. solmelia.com** 🕐 **All year**

Palacio Ca Sa Galesa (€€€)
A beautifully restored 17th-century house between the cathedral and the Arab baths. Rooftop terrace and the only indoor pool in the old city.
✉ **Carrer de Miramar 8**

☎ **971 715400; www.palacio casagalesa.com** 🕐 **All year**

Palau Sa Font (€€€)
A 16th-century palace converted into a boutique hotel, with pink walls, wooden floors and a small terrace pool.
✉ **Carrer dels Apuntadors 38**
☎ **971 712277; www.palausa font.com** 🕐 **All year**

Portixol (€€€)
Scandinavian design meets fifties architecture at this seaside hotel in an up-and-coming harbour district.
✉ **Carrer Sirena 27** ☎ **971 271800; www.portixol.com** 🕐 **All year**

Puro (€€€)
Palma's latest boutique hotel, opened in 2004 in a restored mansion.
✉ **Carrer Montenegro 12**
☎ **971 425450; www.puro hotel.com** 🕐 **All year**

Ritzi (€)
Budget *hostal* centrally located for Palma's *tapas* and nightlife quarter.
✉ **Carrer Apuntadors 6**
☎ **971 714610** 🕐 **All year**

San Lorenzo (€€)
Six rooms only in a restored 17th-century manor house, with a rooftop swimming pool and attractive garden, close to the old city.
✉ **Carrer Sant Llorenç 14**
☎ **971 728200; www.hotel sanlorenzo.com** 🕐 **All year**

Son Vida (€€€)
Exclusive hotel in a 13th-century castle with golf course, 5km north of Palma.
✉ **Urbanización Son Vida**
☎ **971 790000; www.hotel sonvida.com** 🕐 **All year**

Around the Island

Alcúdia

Es Convent (€€€)
Four tastefully decorated rooms in a pair of stone houses in the heart of the old town.

✉ Carrer Progrès 6 ☎ 971 548716; www.esconvent.com

🕐 Feb–Nov

Algaida

Raims (€€)
Rural apartments around the courtyard of a 17th-century manor house. Breakfast is taken in a delightful garden of palm trees.

✉ Carrer Ribera 21

☎ 971 665157; www.finca-raims.com 🕐 All year

Artà

Ca'n Moragues (€€)
Just eight rooms and a heated swimming pool and sauna in this stylish renovated town house.

✉ Carrer Pou Nou 12 ☎ 971 829509; www.canmoragues.com

🕐 All year

Banyalbufar

Baronía (€)
Two-star *hostal* in a former mansion with courtyard, watchtower, swimming pool and sea views.

✉ Carrer Baronía 16

☎ 971 618146 🕐 Apr–Oct

Mar i Vent (€€)
Wonderful views from the terrace of this family-run hotel. Swimming pool and tennis court.

✉ Carrer Major 49

☎ 971 618000; www.hotel marivent.com 🕐 Feb–Nov

Binibona

Ca'n Furiós (€€€)
Cosy British-run farmhouse hotel in a tiny hamlet that is becoming a centre for agrotourism.

✉ Camí Vell Binibona ☎ 971 515751; www.can-furios.com

🕐 Feb–Nov

Es Castell (€€€)
Rustic stone farmhouse surrounded by olive groves, with magnificent views from the terrace. Swimming pool and excellent dinners.

✉ Binibona ☎ 971 875154; www.fincaescastell.com

🕐 All year

Binissalem

Scott's (€€€)
Discreet American-owned hotel, all antique furniture and Persian rugs, in a 19th-century town house on the church square.

✉ Plaça Església 12 ☎ 971 870100; www.scottshotel.com

🕐 All year

Cala Figuera

Villa Serena (€)
Simple two-star hotel, perfectly situated at the mouth of a pretty bay.

✉ Carrer Virgen del Carmen 37

☎ 971 645303 🕐 Apr–Oct

Cala Rajada

Ses Rotges (€€)
An old-style villa with a beautiful flower-filled garden and a Michelin-starred restaurant.

✉ Carrer Rafael Blanes 21

☎ 971 563108 🕐 Apr–Oct

Cala Sant Vicenç

Cala Sant Vicenç (€€€)
This family-run seaside hotel near Pollença moved into the luxury bracket after a major renovation in 1996. Facilities include a sauna, gym and a heated outdoor pool.

✉ Carrer Maressers 2

☎ 971 530250 🕐 Feb–Nov

Reis de Mallorca

Reis de Mallorca (Kings of Mallorca) is an independent group of 30 Mallorcan hotels. It includes some of the best hotels on the island, like Palacio Ca Sa Galesa in Palma, L'Hermitage in Orient and Illa d'Or in Porta de Pollença, but also cheaper options like the Mar i Vent in Banyalbufar. What they all have in common is individuality, architectural beauty and generally excellent cuisine. Reis de Mallorca hotels can be booked on ☎ 971 770737; www.reisdemallorca.com.

Monasteries

Several of Mallorca's former monasteries rent out old monks' and pilgrims' cells to travellers. You may not get a shower but you will find peace, a sense of history and unforgettable hilltop views. The best known, at Lluc, is now virtually a hotel; for real solitude head instead for the Ermita de Bonany (➤ 55), Puig de Maria (➤ 74) or the sanctuary above Castell d'Alaró (➤ 19).

Deià
La Residencia (€€€)
A pair of 16th-century *fincas* with terraced orchards converted into a luxury hotel, considered by many to be the best on the island. Four-poster beds in every suite.
✉ **Finca Son Canals** ☎ 971 639011; www.hotel-lasresidencia.com ⏱ Feb–Nov

Sa Pedrissa (€€)
Eight rooms and suites in a 17th-century farmhouse with stunning views.
✉ **Carretera Valldemossa-Deià** ☎ 971 639111; www.sapedrissa.com ⏱ All year

S'Hotel d'Es Puig (€€)
The 'hotel on the hill' featured in a short story by Robert Graves and also in Gordon West's *Jogging Round Majorca*.
✉ **Carrer Es Puig 4** ☎ 971 639409; www.hoteldespuig.com ⏱ All year

Formentor
Hotel Formentor (€€€)
This was Mallorca's first luxury hotel outside Palma when it opened in 1929. It is a grand hotel in a beautiful setting between the beach and the pine woods, with acres of terraced gardens.
✉ **Platja de Formentor** ☎ 971 899100; www.hotelformentor.net ⏱ Apr–Oct

Fornalutx
Ca'n Verdera (€€€)
An old stone house has been tastefully converted into a modern boutique hotel, a great place to relax among the orange groves once the day trippers have left.
✉ **Carrer de Toros 1** ☎ 971 638203; www.canverdera.com ⏱ All year

Lluc
Monestir de Lluc (€)
Comfortable accommodation in a former monastery – a popular base for walking in the Serra de Tramuntana.
✉ **Lluc monastery** ☎ 971 871525 ⏱ All year

Lluc-Alcari
Costa d'Or (€€)
Simple but perfect, in a magical setting above the sea. You can walk to the shore through the hotel's own pine forest.
✉ **Lluc-Alcari** ☎ 971 639025; www.hoposa.es ⏱ Apr–Oct

Manacor
La Reserva Rotana (€€€)
This 17th-century mansion with its own golf course is typical of the new breed of upmarket rural hotels that are opening up in Mallorca.
✉ **Camí de S'Avall, km3** ☎ 971 845685; www.la-reserva-rotana.com ⏱ Feb–Nov

Orient
Dalt Muntanya (€€)
A former walkers' hostel, recently renovated as part of the trend towards upmarket rural tourism.
✉ **Carretera de Bunyola** ☎ 971 615373 ⏱ All year

L'Hermitage (€€€)
Former convent turned into a country-house hotel, with swimming pool, tennis courts, sauna and a first-class restaurant.
✉ **Carretera Alaró–Bunyola** ☎ 971 180303; www.hermitage-hotel.com ⏱ Feb–Nov

Petra
Sa Plaça (€€)
If you want to get away from

it all in an authentic Mallorcan village, stay in one of the three rooms in this town house on the main square.

📧 **Plaça Ramón Llull 4**
📞 **971 561646** 🕐 **Closed Nov**

Pollença
Juma (€€)
This early 20th-century hotel on the main square has recently reopened its doors to cater for the growing numbers of people wanting to stay in inland towns. Eight comfortable rooms, decorated in antique style.

📧 **Plaça Major 9**
📞 **971 535002;**
www.hoteljuma.com
🕐 **All year**

Port de Pollença
Illa d'Or (€€)
Charming old-fashioned beach hotel at the end of the promenade.

📧 **Passeig Colón 265**
📞 **971 865100; www.hoposa.es**
🕐 **Feb–Nov**

Port de Sóller
Es Port (€€)
Three-star family-run *hostal* in a 15th-century mansion with a private chapel in the courtyard. The bar has the biggest olive press you'll ever see.

📧 **Carrer Antoni Montis**
📞 **971 631650** 🕐 **Feb–Nov**

Sant Elm
Hostal Dragonera (€)
Simple but comfortable beachside hotel with a sun terrace right by the sea and magical views of Dragonera. The hotel can arrange bike hire, walks and horse-riding for guests.

📧 **Avinguda Rei Jaume I 5**
📞 **971 239086** 🕐 **Feb–Nov**

Santa Maria del Camí
Read's (€€€)
British-run hotel and sophisticated restaurant in a magnificent restored *finca* on the road to Alaró.

📧 **Carretera Santa Maria–Alaró** 📞 **971 140261; www. readshotel.com** 🕐 **All year**

Ses Illetes
Bon Sol (€€€)
Delightful family-run hotel, arranged like a wedding-cake on several levels and cascading down a hill, culminating in its own private beach.

📧 **Passeig Illetes 30** 📞 **971 402111** 🕐 **Closed Nov**

Sineu
Son Cleda (€€€)
Attractive three-star hotel in a restored 17th-century house overlooking the market square.

📧 **Plaça Es Fossar 7** 📞 **971 521040** 🕐 **All year**

Sóller
Ca N'Ai (€€€)
Four-star *hotel rural* in a manor house surrounded by orange groves.

📧 **Camí Son Sales 50** 📞 **971 632494** 🕐 **Feb–Oct**

El Guía (€)
Old-style hotel/restaurant by the station giving excellent value for money.

📧 **Carrer Castanyer 2** 📞 **971 630227** 🕐 **Apr–Oct**

Valldemossa
Ca'n Mario (€)
Charming family-run *hostal* filled with antiques. There is a good restaurant on the first floor.

📧 **Carrer Uetam 8**
📞 **971 612122** 🕐 **All year**

Fincas
Many of Mallorca's *fincas* (country estates) have recently been converted into upmarket tourist accommodation, combining character (stone farmhouses, antiques and beautiful views) with modern amenities like swimming pools. You can get information on *fincas* from the Associació Agroturisme Balear, Avinguda de Gabriel Alomar i Villalonga 8a, Palma (📞 971 721508; www.topfincas.com) or from the independent association (www.fincaturismo.com).

Grand Hotel Sóller
Sóller's first tourist hotel reopened in 2004 as a luxury hotel and spa resort, with views over the town and mountains from the rooftop pool and terrace.

📧 Carrer Romaguera 18
📞 971 721508
🕐 All year

Markets

Weekly Markets

Almost every town in Mallorca has a weekly market; most start early and wind up by lunchtime. The larger markets all follow a similar pattern – fresh produce around the main square, specialist food stalls fanning out from there, then cheap clothes, household goods and craft stalls for the tourists. The biggest market is on Thursdays at Inca; the most traditional is the Wednesday agricultural and livestock market at Sineu.

Palma

Llotja del Peix (Fish Market)

Get here early as the night's catch goes on sale and mullet, prawns, sardines and sea bass are hawked by women with operatic voices.

- ✉ Es Moll de Pescadors
- 🕐 Mon–Sat 6AM

Mercat Artesanal

Lively craft market on the Plaça Major, with buskers and open-air cafés.

- ✉ Plaça Major 🕐 Mon–Sat 10–8 in summer; Fri, Sat only in winter

Mercat Olivar

Palma's main market, in a hall near Plaça d'Espanya. Meat, fish and fresh produce on the ground floor, and a supermarket upstairs (▶ 37).

- ✉ Plaça Olivar ☎ 971 720315 🕐 Mon–Sat 8–2

Rambla

It may not match its Barcelona namesake, but Palma's Rambla is similarly lined with flower stalls.

- ✉ Passeig de la Rambla
- 🕐 Mon–Fri 8–2, 5–8, Sat 8–2

Rastro (Flea Market)

A Palma institution which takes over part of the main ring road each Saturday morning. Plenty of bargains but lots of junk too.

- ✉ Avinguda de Gabriel Alomar i Villalonga 🕐 Sat 8–2

Santa Catalina

Fresh fruit and vegetable market just west of the city centre, in the district of the same name. This is where some of Palma's top chefs come to do their shopping. As well as fresh produce, meat and fish, the market also has delicatesen stalls specialising in wine, oils, vinegars and sushi.

- ✉ Plaça Navegació
- 🕐 Mon-Sat 8-2

Weekly Markets Outside Palma

Alaró – Sat

Alcúdia – Tue, Sun

Algaida – Fri

Andratx – Wed

Artà – Tue

Binissalem – Fri

Cala Rajada – Sat

Calvià – Mon

Campos – Thu, Sat

Capdepera – Wed

Colònia de Sant Jordi – Wed

Felanitx – Sun

Inca – Thu

Llucmajor – Wed, Sun

Manacor – Mon

Montuïri – Mon

Muro – Sun

Petra – Wed

Pollença – Sun

Porreres – Tue

Port de Pollença – Wed

Porto Cristo – Sun

Pòrtol – Thu

Santa Eugènia – Sat

Santa Maria del Camí – Sun

Santanyí – Wed, Sat

S'Arenal – Thu

Ses Salines – Thu

Sineu – Wed

Sóller – Sat

Valldemossa – Sun

Vilafranca de Bonany – Wed

Shopping in Palma

Shopping Districts

The main shopping areas in Palma are Avinguda Jaume III for upmarket boutiques (leather, antiques, designer clothes) and the pedestrian streets around Plaça Major for small specialist shops. There is also a modern shopping mall and hypermarket complex, Centro Comercial Porto Pi, 2km from the centre.

Books

La Casa del Mapa
Books and maps about Mallorca.
✉ **Carrer Sant Domingo 11**
☎ **971 225944**

Ereso
A good selection of books about Mallorca in English and German.
✉ **Carrer Paraires 1**
☎ **971 710283**

Fiol
Palma's leading second-hand bookshop.
✉ **Carrer Oms 45**
☎ **971 721428**

Fundació la Caixa
Art books and posters in the ground floor of this modern art gallery.
✉ **Plaça Weyler 3**
☎ **971 728071** 🕐 **Mon–Sat 10–9, Sun 10–2**

Ripoll
Antiquarian books and prints.
✉ **Carrer Sant Miquel 12**
☎ **971 721355**

Department Stores

El Corte Inglés
Branches of Spain's leading department store. The Club del Gourmet has Spanish wines, hams and cheeses.
✉ **Avinguda Jaume III 15; Avinguda Alexandre Rosselló 12**
☎ **971 770177** 🕐 **Mon–Sat 9:30–9:30**

Food & Wine

Bon Vins
Excellent selection of Mallorcan and Spanish wines and olive oils.
✉ **Carrer Sant Feliu 7**
☎ **971 214041**

Colmado Santo Domingo
Fight your way past hundreds of hanging *sobrasada* sausages to find cheeses, fig cake and olive oil.
✉ **Carrer Sant Domingo 1**
☎ **971 714887**

Forn d'es Teatre
Art nouveau shopfront and the place to buy *ensaimadas*.
✉ **Plaça Weyler 9**
☎ **971 715254**

Forn Fondo
Bakery which has turned out *ensaimadas* since 1911.
✉ **Carrer Unió 15** ☎ **971 711634**

Frasquet
Go in here just to smell the melted chocolate.
✉ **Carrer Brossa 19**
☎ **971 721354**

La Montaña
Sausages, hams, cheeses and one of Palma's best window displays.
✉ **Carrer Jaume II 27** ☎ **971 712595**

Son Vivot
Mallorcan and Menorcan produce, including *sobrasada*, cheese and wine.
✉ **Plaça Porta Pintada 1**
☎ **971 720748**

Shopping Tips

Most shops are open from around 10 to 1:30 and 5 to 8 Monday to Friday, and on Saturday mornings. The exceptions are souvenir shops in the large resorts, which stay open every day, and the larger supermarkets, which open throughout the day Monday to Saturday. Most shops accept credit cards, but it is always advisable to have some cash.

Arts & Crafts

Siurells
Siurells are clay whistles, which have been made on Mallorca since Arab times. They come in all shapes and sizes – the most common design is a man on horseback – and are painted white with flashes of red and green. They are cheap, children love them, and the artist Joan Miró was much influenced by their brightness and simplicity.

Craft Fairs
A *Fira del Fang* (Ceramics Fair) is held each March in the town of Marratxí and all of Mallorca's leading potters are represented. Prices here are much better than in the tourist shops. *Baleart* is a Christmas craft fair held in Palma each December, with stalls selling everything from pottery and handmade shoes to Mallorcan wines and *sobrasada* sausages.

Palma
Alpargatería Llinas
The best place to buy espadrilles (rope-soled shoes).
✉ **Carrer Sant Miquel 43**
☎ **971 717696**

Camper
Camper shoes are both funky and functional and this Mallorcan firm has become a global brand. There are other branches on Avinguda Jaume III, at Porto Pí and at the airport, as well as factory outlet stores at Inca and Festival Park (► facing page).
✉ **Carrer Sant Miquel 17**
☎ **971 726254**

La Casa del Olivo
Wonderful olive-carver's workshop in an alley off Carrer Jaume II. The best buy here is salad bowls – they're not cheap but you're paying for old-fashioned craftsmanship.
✉ **Carrer Pescatería Vella 4**
☎ **971 727025**

Fang i Foc
A good range of ceramics from Mallorca and the Spanish mainland.
✉ **Carrer Libertat 29**
☎ **971 455860**

Fet a Mà
As the name implies, everything 'made by hand'. Pottery and glass, both traditional and modern.
✉ **Carrer Sant Miquel 52**
☎ **971 711095**

Herreros de Vicente Juan Ribas
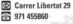
The best place to buy *roba de llengues*, patterned cloth made on the island for over a century. There is another *roba de llengues* shop, Juncosa, in the same street.

✉ **Carrer Sant Nicolau 10**
☎ **971 721773**

Majórica
Palma branches of Mallorca's leading artificial-pearl-maker.
✉ **Avinguda Jaume III 11; Plaça Mercat 9** ☎ **971 725268; 971 722919**

Midge Dalton
Palma's antique shops are perfect for browsing, and this is one of the best.
✉ **Plaça Mercat 20**
☎ **971 713360**

Natura
Mallorcan branch of a Spanish chain specialising in environment-friendly gifts – candles, wood, clothes.
✉ **Passeig des Born 9**
☎ **971 718252**

Passeig per l'Artesania
A complex of craft shops and workshops set in an old factory, where artists sell woodwork, pottery, glassware, paperwork, recycled goods, food and wine – all made in Mallorca.
✉ **Plaça Llorenç Bisbal Batle**
☎ **971 717717**

Persépolis
High-class antiques on Palma's upmarket shopping street.
✉ **Avinguda Jaume III 23**
☎ **971 724539**

S'Avarca
Traditional Menorcan handmade sandals.
✉ **Carrer Sant Domingo 14**
☎ **971 712058**

Vidrierías Gordiola
The best choice of Algaida glassware in Palma.
✉ **Carrer Victoria 2** ☎ **971 711541**

Around the Island

Algaida
Vidrierías Gordiola
Glass factory and museum
(► 43) in a mock castle near
Algaida.
✉ **Carretera Palma–Manacor,
km19** ☎ **971 665046**

Felantx
Ceramiques Felanitx
A large selection of local
pottery at competitive prices,
including simple brown-glazed
plates, pots and bowls.
✉ **Carrer Major 12**
☎ **971 580395**

Inca
Munper
Mallorcan leather is rarely a
bargain these days, but this
is the place to go for a wide
selection of shoes, handbags
and belts – the factory has
another shop at Montuïri.
✉ **Carretera Palma–Alcúdia,
km30** ☎ **971 881000**

Manacor
Majórica
Shop here after touring
Mallorca's largest pearl
factory (► 60).
✉ **Avinguda Majórica 48**
☎ **971 550200**

OlivArt
Emporium where everything
is made from olive wood.
✉ **Carretera Palma–Manacor,
km45** ☎ **971 552800**

Montuïri
Orquídea
Large factory shop featuring
artificial pearls.
✉ **Carretera Palma–Manacor,
km30** ☎ **971 644144**

Pòrtol
Ca's Canonge
Large selection of pottery,

especially heavy brown-
glazed cooking pots.
✉ **Carrer Ca's Canonge 41**
☎ **971 602361**

Ca Madò Bet
The lovely hand-made and
painted *siurells* (► 106) are
produced in a local village
house.
✉ **Carrer Jaume I 10, Sa
Cabaneta** ☎ **971 602156**

Roca Llisa
One of the best places to
buy *siurells* (► 106).
✉ **Carrer Roca Llisa 24**
☎ **971 602497**

Santa Maria del Camí
Ca'n Bernat
Master craftsman's
workshop turning out
imaginative local pottery.
✉ **Carrer Bartomeu Pasqual**
☎ **971 621306**

Santanyí
Ceramiques de Santanyí
Innovative ceramic designs
based on ancient Mallorcan
traditions.
✉ **Carrer Guardia Civil 22**
☎ **971 163128**

Sóller
Eugenio
Gifts carved out of olive
wood – salad bowls,
salt-cellars, chess sets.
✉ **Carrer Jerónimo Estades
11A** ☎ **971 630984**

Fet a Sóller
The shop inside the station
sells local produce and
crafts, including olive oil, ice
cream and orange
marmalade. Profits go to a
local workshop for disabled
people.
✉ **Estació de Sóller** ☎ **971
633942**

Wine
Mallorcan wines have
been growing in reputation
in recent years and several
bodegas sell direct to the
public. If you are lucky you
will be able to taste before
you buy. Among the best
producers are José
L Ferrer at Binissalem
(☎ 971 511050), Miquel
Oliver at Petra (☎ 971
561117) and Jaume
Mesquida at Porreres
(☎ 971 647106).

Factory Outlets
There are numerous
factory shops selling
leather, pearls and
glassware on the main
roads across the island.
One of the best is
RECamper, an outlet store
for Camper shoes in a
warehouse off the Inca
bypass. Camper also have
an outlet store at Festival
Park, an American-style
mall off the Palma-Inca
motorway, with fast-food
restaurants, cinemas and
the Green Planet
reptilarium.

Parks, Zoos & Activities

Family Outings

As well as the attractions listed here, children will enjoy visits to La Granja (➤ 57) and to the various caves along the east coast with their phantasmagorical light displays (➤ 21, 54). The Sóller train and tram ride (➤ 71) makes a fun day out, and the beach at Platja de Palma (➤ 64) is very child-friendly with its seafront 'train', shallow water and Red Cross beach stations. Another enjoyable activity for children is a ride around Palma on a *galera* (horse-drawn carriage). You can pick one up from the top of Costa de la Seu, beside the cathedral and Palau de L'Almudaina.

A Warning

The attractions listed on this page are among the most expensive in Mallorca.

Mallorca is well geared up for family holidays. There are lots of good sandy beaches with safe, shallow water and first-aid stations, and many of the resorts have crazy golf courses and pony rides. Some hotels have children's pools and many also offer nurseries and baby-sitting services, as well as children's entertainment. If this is important to you, check with your hotel or travel agent before you go.

Here is a selection of activities that will appeal to children.

Theme Parks

Magaluf
Western Park

'Crazy Wet West' is the slogan of this Wild West theme park, with cowboy and high-diving shows, thrilling water rides, playgrounds, fast food and video arcades.

🖂 Carretera Cala Figuera ☎ 971 131203 🕓 May–Oct, daily 10–6

Waterparks

Magaluf
Aquapark

There are pools, slides, a 'water castle' and exciting rides at this waterpark on the edge of town.

🖂 Carretera Cala Figuera ☎ 971 131203 🕓 May–Oct, daily 10–6

Port d'Alcùdia
Hidropark

A water-based theme park with activities for very young children, as well as waterslides, wave pools and mini-golf.

🖂 Avinguda Tucán ☎ 971 891672 🕓 May–Oct, daily 10–6

S'Arenal (Platja de Palma)
Aquacity

One of the world's largest water funfairs, with enough thrills and spills to keep little ones happy all day.

🖂 End of Palma–S'Arenal motorway ☎ 971 440000 🕓 May–Sep, daily 10–5; Oct, Sun–Fri 10–5 🚌 23 from Palma via Platja de Palma

Zoos and Animals

Cala Millor
Safari-Zoo

Drive-round safari park with giraffes, zebra and monkeys plus a 'baby zoo' with young elephants and reptiles born at the zoo (➤ 45). Arrive early to see the animals feeding.

🖂 Carretera Porto Cristo–Son Servera, km5 ☎ 971 810909 🕓 Apr–Sep, daily 9–7; Oct–Mar, daily 9–5 🚌 Free bus service from Cala Millor in summer

Costitx
Casa de la Fauna Ibero-Balear

Natural history museum containing stuffed animals, birds and fish from Mallorca, Spain and beyond.

🖂 Casa de la Cultura ☎ 971 876070 🕓 Tue-Fri 9-1; also 2nd and 4th Sat and Sun of each month. Closed Aug

Magaluf
Nemo Submarines

See the flora and fauna beneath the sea on a 2-hour exploration by mini-submarine from Magaluf. Very expensive.

✉ Carrer Galéon 2 ☎ 971 130244 🕐 Mar–Oct, daily

Marratxí
Green Planet

Reptilarium featuring snakes, crocodiles, tortoises and iguanas in a modern shopping and entertainment complex.

✉ Festival Park, off the Palma-Inca motorway ☎ 971 605481 🕐 Mon-Thu 10-6, Fri-Sun 10-8

Portals Nous
Marineland

The entertainment here is provided by the performing dolphins, sea lions and parrots. There is also a penguin pool, a reptile house and a large collection of sharks and tropical fish, plus flamingoes, monkeys and an impressive aviary. Children can take a ride on a mock pirate boat and a miniature train. The little ones will love it, but their parents may not – especially if they are fond of dolphins. But whatever you think about animal shows, Marineland is a success – and the crowds it attracts mean that it is generating handsome profits, which are then put back into conservation programmes.

✉ Carretera Palma–Andratx, km10 ☎ 971 675125 🕐 Apr–Sep, daily 9:30–6; Oct–Mar, daily 9:30–5. Closed mid-Nov to Christmas 🚌 From Palma, Palma Nova, Magaluf and Santa Ponça

Porto Cristo
Acuàrium de Mallorca

Small aquarium with exotic fish from around the world including piranhas and electric eels. Next to the Coves del Drac (▶ 54).

✉ Carrer Vèlla ☎ 971 820971 🕐 Apr–Oct, daily 10:30–6; Nov–Mar, daily 11–3

Santa Eugènia
Natura Parc

An easy walking trail leads around a wildlife park where Mallorcan farm animals can be seen, along with butterflies, black vultures and imported species like pelicans and Chinese geese. Picnic area and café.

✉ Carretera de Sineu, km15 ☎ 971 144078 🕐 Apr–Oct, daily 10–7; Nov–Mar, daily 10–5

Mini Golf

Palma Nova
Golf Fantasia

There are mini-golf courses in many of the resorts, but this is one of the best, set amid waterfalls, caves and tropical gardens. There is a choice of 3 different circuits – or you can play all 54 holes. Even adults will enjoy it.

✉ Carrer Tenis 3, Palma Nova ☎ 971 135040 🕐 Daily, 10AM–midnight

Golf Paradis

Three different courses in a fantasy landscape of waterfalls, palm trees and lakes. Also boat rides for kids.

✉ Avinguda de las Lilas ☎ 971 811002 🕐 Daily 10–10 in summer, 10–6 in winter

Museums

Sa Pobla
Ca'n Planes

The top floor has childhood toys and games, while the lower floor houses a contemporary art museum.

✉ Carrer Antoni Maura 6 ☎ 971 542389 🕐 Tue–Sat 10–2, 4–8, Sun 10–2

Looking After Children

Small children are particularly vulnerable to sun and need to be well protected: apply a high-factor sun block regularly, especially after swimming. If you need a child seat in your rented car, be sure to book it in advance and then check it carefully on arrival. The same goes for cots and high-chairs in hotels and apartments. Finally, don't forget to check that your balcony railings are secure.

109

Theatres & Concerts

What's On?
To find out what's on while you are staying, ask any tourist office for a copy of *Where To Go*, published quarterly in English and German. The *Majorca Daily Bulletin* also has daily listings. A monthly guide to events in Palma is published in Spanish and Catalan and available at tourist offices and hotels. Remember that everything starts late in Mallorca – opera at 9PM, theatre around 10PM and music any time up to midnight.

Cinema
To see films in their original language soon after release, check out the multiplex cinemas at Festival Park, off the Palma to Inca motorway (☎ 902 999686). There is another large cinema complex, showing Spanish and international films, at the Porto Pí centre, 2km west of Palma (☎ 971 405500).

Palma
Auditòrium
Palma's main venue for theatre and concerts.
✉ **Passeig Marítim 18**
☎ **971 735328**

Castell de Bellver
Outdoor classical concerts on summer evenings.
✉ **Parc Bellver**

Centre de Cultura Sa Nostra
A programme of free events is presented at this arts centre in an old mansion in central Palma.
✉ **Carrer Concepció 12**
☎ **971 725210**

Parc de la Mar
Free outdoor concerts (jazz, rock or classical) beneath the city walls in summer.
✉ **Parc de la Mar**

Teatre Municipal
Contemporary drama, dance, ballet and films.
✉ **Passeig Mallorca 9**
☎ **971 739148**

Teatre Sans
Cutting-edge drama in Catalan at back-street fringe theatre.
✉ **Carrer Ca'n Sanç 5**
☎ **971 727266**

Teatre Xesc Forteza
Contemporary drama and music in a new theatre, which opened in 2003.
✉ **Plaça Prevere Miquel Maura 1** ☎ **971 720135**

Around the Island

Alcúdia
Auditori d'Alcúdia
A stunning new hall hosting concerts and drama.
✉ **Plaça de la Porta de Mallorca 3** ☎ **971 897185**

Cala Millor
Sa Màniga
New auditorium with regular concerts and exhibitions.
✉ **Carrer Son Galta 4**
☎ **971 587373**

Deià
Son Marroig
Concerts on summer evenings in the gardens created by Archduke Ludwig Salvator. Venue for Deià's classical music festival.
✉ **Carretera Valldemossa– Deià** ☎ **971 639178**

Esporles
La Granja
Displays of folk music and dancing on Wednesday and Friday afternoons at this museum of Mallorcan traditions (▶ 57).
✉ **La Granja**
☎ **971 610032**

Pollença
Convent Sant Domingo
The cloisters of this 17th-century monastery make a delightful setting for Pollença's international music festival (summer).
✉ **Carrer Sant Domingo**
☎ **971 534012;**
www.festivalpollenca.org

Valldemossa
Reial Cartoixa
Chopin festival held each August in the Carthusian monastery.
✉ **Valldemossa**
☎ **971 612351;**
www.festivalchopin.com

Costa Nord
Top names in flamenco, salsa and jazz perform here during the Mediterranean Nights Festival (summer).
✉ **Avinguda Palma 6**
☎ **971 612425**

Bars

Resort Bars

Bars in the main resorts change their names and identities so frequently that recommendations are useless – follow your nose and you will soon find one that you like. Many bars are foreign-owned, with German or British names, imported beer and satellite TV. A stretch of the Platja de Palma is known as *carrer de la cervesa* ('Beer Street') owing to the number of German bars; the British equivalent is in Magaluf.

Palma

The best places for late-night bar-hopping are in the streets around Plaça de la Llotja and the terrace bars along the waterfront on Passeig Marítim.

Abaco

Palma's most unusual bar – in a 17th-century palace close to La Llotja (➤ panel).
✉ **Carrer Sant Joan 1**
☎ **971 714939** 🕐 **8PM–3AM**

Atlantico

Popular American-themed old town bar with a wide range of cocktails.
✉ **Carrer Sant Feliu 12** ☎ **971 728986** 🕐 **8PM–3AM**

Barcelona

Cool jazz bar in a basement beside Abaco.
✉ **Carrer Apuntadors 5**
☎ **971 713557** 🕐 **From 9PM; live jazz from 10PM nightly**

Cappuccino Grand Café

The hippest meeting place in town in an old Renaissance palace with a shady courtyard and art gallery.
✉ **Carrer Sant Miquel 53**
☎ **971 719764** 🕐 **8AM–1AM**

Cappuccino Grand Café

The original Cappuccino Grand Café, on the waterfront, is still a popular place to meet for coffee or late-night cocktails.
✉ **Passeig Marítim 1**
☎ **971 282162** 🕐 **8:30AM–3AM**

Dàrsena

Fashionable waterfront terrace bar. Great location.
✉ **Passeig Marítim** ☎ **971 180504** 🕐 **Mon–Sat 8AM–midnight, Sun 8AM–9PM**

Havana Moon

Trendiest of the bars by the ritzy Puerto Portals marina.
✉ **Puerto Portals** ☎ **971 677522** 🕐 **5PM–4AM**

Hogans

Palma's first Irish pub opened in 1996. Occasional Irish fiddling, popular with locals.
✉ **Carrer Monsenyor Palmer 2**
☎ **971 289664** 🕐 **Noon–3AM**

El Pesquero

Former fishermen's bar, now a chic waterfront café with *tapas*, drinks and harbour views from a terrace.
✉ **Moll de la Llotja 2**
☎ **971 721079** 🕐 **7:30AM–late**

Varadero

Trendy terrace bar at the end of the old quay, with great views of the cathedral when it is floodlit at night.
✉ **Moll Vell** ☎ **971 726428**
🕐 **9AM–late**

Near Palma
Abacanto

Cousin of Abaco in a 19th-century mansion in the suburb of S'Indioteria. It is difficult to find – take a taxi.
✉ **Camí Son Nicolau, S'Indioteria** ☎ **971 430624**
🕐 **9PM–2AM**

Abaco

Push open a heavy wooden door in Palma's busy nightlife quarter and you enter a different world. Huge baskets of fruit cascade onto the floor; there are fresh flowers everywhere and a subtle hint of incense. You sip fruit cocktails by candlelight, while listening to classical music, then wander into the courtyard with its fountains and caged birds. The drinks are expensive, but everyone should go once.

Discos & Dinner Shows

Dinner Shows

A recent arrival in Mallorca is the 'themed' dinner show and spectacle, which can be anything from folklore and flamenco dancing to a medieval banquet complete with jousting and serving wenches. These shows are basically aimed at tour groups; you can book at any resort hotel. Don't go unless you are prepared to abandon your inhibitions and join in the fun.

Discos

Palma

Mar Salada

Cool late-night disco right on the harbour, within the Club de Mar.

✉ **Moll de Pelaires** ☎ 971 702709 ⏰ Fri–Sat 11PM–6AM

Pacha

Young and trendy club where Palma's teenagers come to bop the night away.

✉ **Passeig Marítim 42** ☎ 971 737788 ⏰ 11PM–6AM; nightly in summer, Thu–Sat in winter

Tito's

Not quite as young as nearby Pacha. There are six bars, a laser show and fantastic views over Palma bay. You enter via an outdoor lift from the seafront promenade.

✉ **Passeig Marítim** ☎ 971 730017 ⏰ 11PM–6AM; Tue–Sun in summer, Thu–Sat in winter

Around the Island

Magaluf

BCM

Europe's largest and probably loudest disco, with laser shows, banks of video screens, a swimming pool and room for 4,000 people. The upper level is for the young-and-trendy crowd, while the over-30s gather downstairs. International stars here throughout the summer season.

✉ **Avinguda S'Olivera** ☎ 971 131546 ⏰ 10PM–5AM; nightly in summer, weekends in winter

Platja de Palma

Rui Palace

Large, loud international disco club with visits from top European DJs in summer.

✉ **Las Maravillas** ☎ 971 743474 ⏰ 11PM–6AM; nightly in summer

Port d'Alcúdia

Menta

Designed like a Roman temple around an open-air pool, it honours Alcúdia's history each May with a 'Roman orgy'.

✉ **Avinguda Argentina** ☎ 971 891972 ⏰ 11PM–6AM; nightly in summer, weekends in winter

Dinner Shows

Around the Island

Bunyola

Son Amar

Spanish dancing, ballet, flamenco, soul music and magic tricks at Mallorca's top cabaret show, in a 16th-century mansion, near Bunyola.

✉ **Carretera Palma–Sóller, km11** ☎ 971 617533 ⏰ Apr–Oct, dinner from 8, show 9

Magaluf

Casino Mallorca

A choice of gambling in the casino (passport and smart dress required) or the Paladium dinner show with dancing.

✉ **Urbanización Sol de Mallorca** ☎ 971 130000 ⏰ Mon–Sat 6PM–4AM, Sun 3PM–4AM ; show Tue, Thu, Fri, Sat 10PM

Pirate Adventure

Yo-ho-ho and a bundle of fun on a mock pirate ship – with lots of audience participation required. Don't say you weren't warned!

✉ **Carretera La Porrassa** ☎ 971 130411 ⏰ May–Oct, Mon–Fri (times vary)

Golf Courses

Palma

Son Vida
Mallorca's first golf course opened in 1964 on an exclusive estate above Palma.

✉ Urbanización Son Vida
☎ 971 799999

Around the Island

Bunyola

Son Termens
Attractive course on an old hunting estate.

✉ Carrer de S'Esglaieta, km10
☎ 971 617862

Cala Millor

Son Servera
Nine-hole course amid pine woods by the sea.

✉ Urbanización Costa dels Pins, 6km from Cala Millor
☎ 971 840096

Camp de Mar

Golf de Andratx
A challenging course with narrow fairways, lakes and sea views.

✉ Carretera Camp de Mar
☎ 971 236280

Capdepera

Canyamel
A testing course with small greens, sloping fairways and sea breezes.

✉ Urbanización Canyamel
☎ 971 841313

Capdepera
Large, fast greens and six lakes, beside the road to Artà.

✉ Carretera Artà–Capdepera
☎ 971 818500

Pula Golf
Challenging course on a luxury golf resort between Capdepera and Cala Millor.

✉ Carretera Son Servera–Capdepera, km3 ☎ 971 817034

Llucmajor

Son Antem
Wide fairways, fast greens and hidden water hazards. A second course opened in 2001.

✉ 3km outside Llucmajor on the PM602 to Palma
☎ 971 129200

Magaluf

Poniente
Long and difficult course, with lots of lakes and bunkers.

✉ Carretera Cala Figuera
☎ 971 130148

Pollença

Pollensa
A tight nine-hole course, with small greens and narrow fairways. If you're golf's not going too well the views from the hill out to sea will make up for it.

✉ 2km outside Pollença on Palma road ☎ 971 533216

Port d'Alcúdia

Alcanada
Mallorca's latest course opened in 2003 in a stunning setting on the Victòria peninsula.

✉ Carretera del Faro
☎ 971 549560

Santa Ponça

Santa Ponça
The venue for the Balearic Open, featuring long, wide fairways in open countryside dotted with almond trees.

✉ Urbanización Golf Santa Ponça ☎ 971 690211

Ses Illetes

Real Golf de Bendinat
Undulating course set among pine woods above the bay of Palma.

✉ Urbanización Bendinat
☎ 971 405200

Golf in Mallorca

In 1976 there were two golf courses in Mallorca; now there are 15 and more are being built. All are open throughout the year, providing a refuge for golfers fleeing frost and winter greens elsewhere. The typical cost of a round is €60–70, though this is much reduced if you come on a golfing package holiday. Don't forget to bring a handicap certificate.

Watersports

Sailing in Mallorca
Mallorca has 42 marinas, 30 *clubs nautics* and mooring for 10,000 yachts. Yachts can be chartered locally and most marinas also have facilities for water-skiing and windsurfing. Highlights of the sailing year include the King's Cup in August, the Princess Sofía trophy at Easter, and the Rei en Jaume regatta in July when a flotilla of yachts re-creates the 185-km journey made by Jaume the Conqueror when he landed at Santa Ponça in 1229.

Sailing

Escuela Nacional de Vela Calanova
The national sailing school in Cala Major runs courses, as well as giving advice on all aspects of sailing in and around Mallorca.
✉ **Avinguda Joan Miró, Cala Major** ☎ **971 402512**

Sail and Surf Pollença
Prestigious sailing club and school on the northeast coast. Instruction is available both for beginners and for the more advanced sailor.
✉ **Passeig Saralegui 134, Port de Pollença** ☎ **971 865346**

Alcúdiamar, Port d'Alcúdia Marina ☎ **971 546000**

Cala d'Or Marina ☎ **971 657070**

Club de Mar, Palma ☎ **971 403611**

Port d'Andratx Marina ☎ **971 671721**

Port de Pollença Marina ☎ **971 864635**

Port de Sóller Marina ☎ **971 633316**

Porto Colom Marina ☎ **971 824658**

Porto Cristo Marina ☎ **971 821253**

Porto Petro Marina ☎ **971 657012**

Puerto Portals Marina (Portals Nous) ☎ **971 171100**

Reial Club Nautic de Palma ☎ **971 726848**

Scuba Diving

Federació Balear de Actividades Subacuáticas
The clear waters around Mallorca are the perfect place for diving, especially in the small, shallow coves of the south and east coasts. The federation is available to give information and advice on all aspects of diving in Mallorca.
✉ **Polideportivo Son Moix, Palma** ☎ **971 288242**

Aqua Marine Diving
✉ **Port d'Andratx**
☎ **971 674376**

Albatros
✉ **Port Cala Bona, Cala Millor**
☎ **971 586807**

Octopus
✉ **Port de Sóller**
☎ **971 633133**

Scuba Activa
✉ **Sant Elm** ☎ **971 239102**

Water-skiing
Water-skiing equipment can be hired on the major beaches, including Cala Millor, Can Picafort, Magaluf, Palma Nova, Peguera, Platja de Palma, Port d'Alcúdia and Santa Ponça.

Windsurfing
There are schools at several of the larger resorts and it is also possible to hire equipment without tuition. Beaches where windsurfing is available include Cala Millor, Cala d'Or, Can Picafort, Magaluf, Palma Nova, Peguera, Platja de Palma, Port d'Alcúdia, Port de Pollença, Port de Sóller, Portals Nous and Santa Ponça.

Spectator Sports

Bullfighting

Bullfighting is considered an art form as much as a sport in Mallorca; the leading *matadors* are national celebrities and there are fights most days on TV. A bullfight begins with a horseback procession, or *corrida*, followed by the fight itself; the bull is softened up by *picadores* and then the *matador* moves in for the kill. Many foreigners detest the spectacle – but it is undoubtedly an important aspect of Spanish culture.

Palma
Plaça de Toros
Bullfights are held in this 1929 bullring between March and October. You can choose between a seat in the sun (*sol*) or the shade (*sombra*).
✉ **Avinguda Gaspar Bennazar Arquitecte** ☎ **971 755245**

Around the Island
Plaça de Toros, Alcúdia
☎ **971 547903**

Plaça de Toros, Felanitx
☎ **971 580557**

Plaça de Toros, Inca
☎ **971 500087**

Plaça de Toros, Muro
This bullring was built in 1910 inside its own quarry of white stone.
☎ **971 537329**

Cricket

Around the Island
Magaluf Cricket Club
Cricket has been kept determinedly going by a group of British ex-pats in Mallorca, who play local and visiting sides on their ground in Magaluf.
☎ **971 233262**

Football

Palma
Son Moix
The home of Real Mallorca FC, who play in the first division and reached the final of the European Cup Winners Cup in 1999. Matches are played on alternate Sunday afternoons between September and June. If you're a keen follower of European football, look out for games involving top Spanish sides like Barcelona and Real Madrid.
✉ **Camí dels Reis**
☎ **971 221221** 🚌 **No. 8**

Horse-racing

Palma
Hipódromo Son Pardo
Europe's first floodlit racecourse opened in 1965. Trotting races (*carreras*) are held around a 1-km track at 4:30 on Sundays in winter and 9 on Friday evenings in summer. Trotting is a form of racing in which the jockey sits in a small cart behind the horse and must prevent the horse from breaking into a gallop. It has been popular in Mallorca and Menorca for at least 200 years. If you go to a horse-race meeting, remember that betting is an essential part of the process.
✉ **Carretera Palma–Sóller, km3** ☎ **971 763853**

Around the Island
Hipódromo Manacor
✉ **Carretera Palma–Artà, km50**
☎ **971 550023**

Tiro Con Honda (Slingshot)
The Roman historian Livy wrote of Balearic slingshot throwers being employed as mercenaries during Hannibal's crossing of the Alps in 218 BC; a statue of a Balearic slinger in the S'Hort del Rei gardens in Palma is a tribute to their importance in Mallorcan history. The art of the slingshot has recently been revived; to see today's slingers, contact the Club de Honderos, ✉ Bar España, Carrer Oms 31, Palma ☎ 971 726250, or check out the website of the Federació Balear de Tir de Fona at www.tirdefona.com

What's On When

Mallorcan Festivals
Find yourself swept along by the atmosphere of a traditional *festa* and you will get a completely different picture of Mallorca. Most are religious in origin and a few date back to the time of the Christian conquest. Every town and village has its saint's day, whose eve (*revelta*) is marked by a *verbena*, a street party with music, dancing, fireworks and fancy dress. Battles are acted out between devils and heroic women, or Christians and Moors; people prance about as horses, and a good time is had by all.

January
Cabalgata de los Reyes Magos (5 Jan): The Three Kings arrive by boat in Palma to distribute gifts to the city's children.
Sant Antoni Abat (16–17 Jan): Processions of pets and farm animals in Palma, Artà and Sa Pobla.
Sant Sebastià (19 Jan): Bonfires and barbecues in Palma's squares.

February
Sa Rúa (final weekend before Lent): Carnival held in Palma and elsewhere on the last weekend before Lent. It is marked by bonfires, fancy dress and processions of decorated floats. In Montuïri the Carnival is known as *Darres Dies* (Last Days).

March/April
Semana Santa (Holy Week): A week of solemn Easter preparation begins on Palm Sunday, when palm and olive branches are blessed at churches across the island before being taken home to adorn front doors. During Holy Week there are processions every day in Palma; the biggest procession is on Maundy Thursday. Other towns and villages have their own processions too. On the evening of Good Friday a figure of Christ is lowered from his cross in Pollença and carried down the Calvary steps in silence. A similar event takes place on the church steps in Felanitx.

May
Moros i Cristians (8–10 May): Mock battles between heroes and infidels in Sóller, commemorating a 1561 battle in which local women helped to defeat a band of Turkish pirates.

June
Sant Pere (28–29 Jun): Processions of fishing boats in Palma, Port d'Andratx and Port d'Alcúdia in honour of the patron saint of fishermen.

July
La Virgen del Carmen (16 Jul): Processions of boats in the island's ports, including Cala Rajada, Port de Pollença and Port de Sóller.
Santa Catalina Thomás (27–28 Jul): Homage to Mallorca's patron saint in her home town of Valldemossa.

August
Sant Bartomeu (24 Aug): Devil-dancing in Montuïri at one of Mallorca's oldest festivals.
Sant Agustí (28 Aug): *Cavallets* dances in Felanitx, with children dressed up as cardboard horses being chased by giants to the accompaniment of bagpipes, flutes and drums.

September/October
Harvest festivals including a melon festival in Vilafranca de Bonany (second Sun in Sep), a wine fair in Binissalem (last Sun in Sep) and a *botifarró* (blood sausage) festival in Sant Joan (third Sun in Oct).

December
Festa de l'Estendard (31 Dec): Palma commemorates the anniversary of the Christian conquest with a procession from the town hall to Mass at the cathedral.

Practical Matters

Above: *Windmill at Algaida;*
Right: *Sóller oranges*

GMT	Mallorca	Germany	USA (NY)	Netherlands	Rest of Spain
12 noon	1PM	1PM	7AM	1PM	1PM

BEFORE YOU GO

WHAT YOU NEED

		UK	Germany	USA	Netherlands	Spain
● Required	Some countries require a passport to remain valid for a minimum period (usually at least six months) beyond the date of entry – contact their consulate or embassy or your travel agent for details.					
○ Suggested						
▲ Not required						
Passport/National Identity Card		●	●	●	●	▲
Visa (Regulations can change – check before planning your journey)		▲	▲	▲	▲	▲
Onward or Return Ticket		○	○	●	○	○
Health Inoculations		▲	▲	▲	▲	▲
Health Documentation (➤ 123, Health)		●	●	●	●	▲
Travel Insurance		○	○	○	○	○
Driving Licence (national with Spanish translation or International)		●	●	●	●	●
Car Insurance Certificate		●	●	●	●	○
Car Registration Document		●	●	●	●	○

WHEN TO GO

Palma

High season

Low season

14°C	15°C	17°C	19°C	22°C	26°C	29°C	29°C	27°C	23°C	18°C	15°C
JAN	FEB	MAR	APR	MAY	JUN	JUL	AUG	SEP	OCT	NOV	DEC

Very wet   Wet   Cloud   Sun   Showers/Sun

TOURIST OFFICES

In the UK
Spanish Tourist Office
79 New Cavendish Street
London
W1W 6XB
☎ 0207 486 8077
Fax: 0207 486 8034
www.spain.info

In the USA
Tourist Office of Spain
666 Fifth Avenue 35th
New York
NY 10103
☎ 212/265 8822
Fax: 212/265 8864
www.okspain.org

POLICE (POLICÍA NACIONAL) 112
FIRE (BOMBEROS) 112
AMBULANCE (AMBULÀNCIA) 112
IN ANY EMERGENCY DIAL 112

WHEN YOU ARE THERE

ARRIVING

Spain's national airline, Iberia, has scheduled flights to Palma's Son Sant Joan Airport from major Spanish and European cities, but charter flights are much cheaper. Ferry services operate from the Spanish mainland, Menorca and Ibiza to Palma.

Son Sant Joan Airport
Kilometres to city centre

8 kilometres

Journey times

🚶 N/A

🚌 30 minutes

🚕 15 minutes

Palma Ferry Terminal
Kilometres to city centre

2 kilometres

Journey times

🚶 N/A

🚌 30 minutes

🚕 10 minutes

MONEY

The euro is the official currency of Spain. Euro banknotes and coins were introduced in January 2002. Banknotes are in denominations of 5, 10, 20, 50, 100, 200 and 500 euros; coins are in denominations of 1, 2, 5, 10, 20 and 50 cents, and 1 and 2 euros. Euro traveller's cheques are widely accepted, as are major credit cards. Credit and debit cards can also be used for withdrawing euro notes from cashpoint machines. Banks can be found in most towns in Mallorca. Spain's former currency, the peseta, went out of circulation in early 2002.

TIME

 Like the rest of Spain, Mallorca is one hour ahead of Greenwich Mean Time (GMT+1), but from late March until late September, summer time (GMT+2) operates.

CUSTOMS

→ **YES**

From another EU country for personal use (guidelines):
800 cigarettes, 200 cigars, 1kg tobacco
10 litres of spirits (over 22%)
20 litres of aperitifs
90 litres of wine, of which 60 litres can be sparkling wine
110 litres of beer
From a non-EU country for your personal use, the allowances are:
200 cigarettes OR 50 cigars OR 250g tobacco
1 litre of spirits (over 22%)
2 litres of intermediary products (eg sherry) and sparkling wine
2 litres of still wine
50g perfume
0.25 litres of eau de toilette
The value limit for goods is €175
Travellers under 17 years of age are not entitled to the tobacco and alcohol allowances

— **NO**

Drugs, firearms, ammunition, offensive weapons, obscene material, unlicensed animals.

119

UK
☎ (971) 712445

Germany
☎ (971) 707737

USA
☎ (971) 403707

Netherlands
☎ (971) 716493

WHEN YOU ARE THERE

TOURIST OFFICES

Mallorca Tourist Board

● Fomento del Turismo de
  Mallorca
  Carrer de Constitució 1
  Palma 07001 ☎ 971 725396

**Local Tourist Offices
(Oficinas de Información
Turística – OIT)**

Palma

● Ca'n Solleric, Passeig des
  Born 27, Palma 07001
  ☎ 971 724090

● Parc de les Estacions
  Palma 07002
  ☎ 971 754329

Palma Nova

● Passeig de la Mar 13
  Calvià 07181
  ☎ 971 682365

Port d'Alcúdia

● Passeig Marítim 68
  Alcúdia 07410
  ☎ 971 547257

Port de Pollença

● Carrer de les Monges 9
  Pollença 07470
  ☎ 971 865467

Sóller

● Plaça d'Espanya
  Sóller 07100
  ☎ 971 638008

Other offices include: Cala
d'Or, Cala Millor, Cala Rajada,
Cala Sant Vicenç, Ca'n
Picafort, Colònia de Sant
Jordi, Magaluf, Peguera,
Platja de Muro, Port de
Sóller, Porto Cristo, S'Arenal,
Ses Illetes and Santa Ponça.

NATIONAL HOLIDAYS

J	F	M	A	M	J	J	A	S	O	N	D
2		(2)	(2)	1			1		1	1	3

1 Jan	New Year's Day
6 Jan	Epiphany
Mar/Apr	Good Friday, Easter Monday
1 May	Labour Day
15 Aug	Assumption of the Virgin
12 Oct	National Day
1 Nov	All Saints' Day
6 Dec	Constitution Day
8 Dec	Feast of the Immaculate Conception
25 Dec	Christmas Day

Many shops and offices close for longer periods
around Christmas and Easter, as well as for the
festivals of Corpus Christi in May/June and Sant
Jaume on 25 July.

OPENING HOURS

○ Shops	● Churches
● Offices	● Museums
● Banks	● Pharmacies

8AM 9AM 10AM 12PM 1PM 2PM 4PM 6PM 8PM

☐ Day	☐ Midday
☐ Evening	

Large department stores, supermarkets and shops in
tourist resorts may open outside the times shown
above, especially in summer. In general, pharmacies,
banks and shops close on Saturday afternoon. Banks
close all day Saturday, June to September, but
stay open until 4:30PM Monday to Thursday, October
to May.

The opening times of museums is just a rough guide;
some are open longer hours in summer while hours
are reduced in winter. Some museums close at
weekends or another day in the week.

DRIVE ON THE
RIGHT

TOILETS
FREE

PUBLIC TRANSPORT

Trains The main railway line connects Palma to Inca, with branch lines to Sa Pobla (via Muro) and Manacor (via Sineu and Petra). There are regular trains throughout the day, taking around 35 minutes to Inca and 1 hour to Manacor (☎ 971 177777). Five trains a day leave Palma for Sóller, beginning at 8AM (☎ 971 752051) and connecting with the tram to Port de Sóller (➤ 71). The two railway stations are found close together in Palma, beside Plaça d'Espanya.

Buses A comprehensive network of buses connects Palma to Mallorca's main towns, with extra services linking the coastal resorts in summer. Buses out of Palma depart from the bus station on Carrer Eusebi Estada, behind Plaça d'Espanya. Palma has its own network of city buses, which also covers the beach resorts around Palma Bay (☎ 971 214444). Bus No 1 runs from 6AM to 2AM between the airport, city centre and port.

Boat Trips In summer there are regular boat tours of Palma Bay and excursions from resorts including Cala d'Or, Port de Pollença and Port de Sóller. Some of these go to remote beaches which can only be reached by boat. There is also the day trip to Cabrera (➤ 46). One trip which runs throughout the year is the journey around the northwest coast from Port de Sóller to Sa Colobra (☎ 971 630170).

Menorca Day trips to Menorca can be made on a fast catamaran, which leaves Cala Rajada at 9AM daily, arriving at the Menorcan city of Ciutadella in one hour. The return journey leaves Ciutadella at 7:30PM (Cape Balear ☎ 902 100444). There are also daily car ferries to Ciutadella from Port d'Alcúdia (☎ 902 119128).

CAR RENTAL

The leading international car rental companies have offices at Palma airport and you can book a car in advance (essential in peak periods) either direct or through a travel agent. Local companies offer competitive rates and will usually deliver a car to the airport.

TAXIS

Taxis can be hired at ranks (indicated by a blue square with a 'T'), on the street (by flagging down those with a green light) or at hotels. They are good value within Palma but expensive over long distances. A list of tariffs is displayed at taxi ranks.

DRIVING

Speed limits on motorways (*autopistas*):
120kph

Speed limits on dual carriageways:
100kph
Speed limits on major roads:
90kph

Speed limits on urban roads:
50kph

Seat belts must be worn at all times. Children under 12 must use a child seat.

Random breath-testing. Never drive under the influence of alcohol.

All hire cars take either unleaded petrol (*sin plomo*) or diesel (*gasoleo*). The top grade is *Super Plus* (98-octane), though *Super* (96-octane) is usually acceptable. Petrol stations are normally open 6AM–10PM, and closed Sundays, though larger ones (often self service) are open 24 hours. Most take credit cards. There are few petrol stations in the mountain areas.

If you break down driving your own car and are a member of an AIT-affiliated motoring club, you can call the Real Automóvil Club de España (☎ 900 118118). If the car is hired follow the instructions given in the documentation; most of the international rental firms provide a rescue service.

PERSONAL SAFETY

The national police force, the Policía Nacional (brown uniforms), keep law and order in urban areas. Some resorts have their own tourist-friendly Policía Turística. If you need a police station ask for *la comisaría*. To help prevent crime:

- Do not carry more cash than you need.
- Do not leave valuables on the beach or poolside.
- Beware of pickpockets in markets, tourist sights or crowded places.
- Avoid walking alone in dark alleys at night.

Police assistance:
☎ **112**
from any call box

TELEPHONES

Most public telephones accept coins, credit cards and telephone cards (*tarjetas telefónicas*), available from post offices, news kiosks and tabacconists. Telephone numbers in Mallorca begin with 971; you must dial all nine digits wherever you are calling from. To call Mallorca from the UK dial 00 34; from the USA dial 011 34. To call the operator dial 002.

International Dialling Codes From Mallorca (Spain) to:	
UK:	00 44
Germany:	00 49
USA:	00 1
Netherlands:	00 31

POST

Post Offices
Post offices are generally open Monday to Friday, 9AM–2PM, but some also open in the afternoon and on Saturday morning. The main post office in Palma at Carrer de Constitució 5 is open Monday to Friday 8:30AM to 8:30PM and Saturday 9AM–2PM ☎ 902 197197

ELECTRICITY

The power supply in Mallorca is: 220–225 volts.

Sockets accept two-round-pin-style plugs, so an adaptor is needed for most non-Continental appliances and a transformer for appliances operating on 100–120 volts.

TIPS/GRATUITIES

Yes ✓ No ✗		
Restaurants (if service not included)	✓	10%
Cafés/bars (if service not included)	✓	change
Tour guides	✓	€1
Hairdressers	✓	change
Taxis	✓	10%
Chambermaids	✓	€1
Porters	✓	€1
Theatre/cinema usherettes	✓	change
Cloakroom attendants	✓	change
Toilets	✗	

📷 **PHOTOGRAPHY**
What to photograph: mountains, hilltop monasteries, pretty mountain villages and attractive harbours.
Best time to photograph: the Mallorcan summer sun can be powerful at the height of the day making photos taken at this time appear 'flat'; it is best to photograph in the early morning or late evening.
Where to buy film: film and camera batteries are readily available from tourist shops and *drouguerias*.

HEALTH

Insurance

Nationals of EU and certain other countries can get medical treatment in Spain with the relevant documentation (Form E111 for Britons), although private medical insurance is still advised and is essential for all other visitors.

Dental Services

Dental treatment is not usually available free of charge as all dentists practise privately. A list of *dentistas* can be found in the yellow pages of the telephone directory. Dental treatment should be covered by private medical insurance.

Sun Advice

The sunniest (and hottest) months are July and August, with an average of 11 hours sun a day and daytime temperatures of 29°C. During these months particularly you should avoid the midday sun and use a strong sunblock.

Drugs

Prescription and non-prescription drugs and medicines are available from pharmacies (*farmàcias*), distinguished by a large green cross. They are able to dispense many drugs which would be available only on prescription in other countries.

Safe Water

Tap water is generally safe though it can be heavily chlorinated. Mineral water is cheap to buy and is sold as *con gas* (carbonated) and *sin gas* (still). Drink plenty of water during hot weather.

CONCESSIONS

Students Holders of an International Student Identity Card may be able to obtain some concessions on travel, entrance fees etc, but Mallorca is not really geared up for students, it is more suited to families and senior citizens. However, there are two youth hostels on the island, one near Palma and the other outside Alcúdia. Another cheap form of accommodation is to stay in a monastery; just turn up or book ahead.

Senior Citizens Mallorca is an excellent destination for older travellers, especially in winter when the resorts are quieter, prices more reasonable and hotels offer very economical long-stay rates. The best deals are available through tour operators who specialise in holidays for senior citizens.

CLOTHING SIZES

Mallorca (Spain)	UK	Rest of Europe	USA		
46	36	46	36		Suits
48	38	48	38		
50	40	50	40		
52	42	52	42		
54	44	54	44		
56	46	56	46		
41	7	41	8		Shoes
42	7.5	42	8.5		
43	8.5	43	9.5		
44	9.5	44	10.5		
45	10.5	45	11.5		
46	11	46	12		
37	14.5	37	14.5		Shirts
38	15	38	15		
39/40	15.5	39/40	15.5		
41	16	41	16		
42	16.5	42	16.5		
43	17	43	17		
34	8	34	6		Dresses
36	10	36	8		
38	12	38	10		
40	14	40	12		
42	16	42	14		
44	18	44	16		
38	4.5	38	6		Shoes
38	5	38	6.5		
39	5.5	39	7		
39	6	39	7.5		
40	6.5	40	8		
41	7	41	8.5		

WHEN DEPARTING

● Remember to contact the airport on the day prior to leaving to ensure the flight details are unchanged.

● If travelling by ferry you must check in no later than the time specified on the ticket.

● Spanish customs officials are usually polite and normally willing to negotiate.

LANGUAGE

The language that you hear on the streets is most likely to be Mallorquín, a version of Catalan, which itself shares features with both French and Spanish but sounds nothing like either and is emphatically a language, not a dialect. Catalan and Spanish both have official status on Mallorca, and though Spanish will certainly get you by (it is still the language used by Mallorcans to address strangers), it is useful to know some Catalan, if only to understand all those street signs which are being slowly replaced in Catalan.

hotel	*hotel*	chambermaid	*cambrera*
bed and breakfast	*llit i berenar*	bath	*bany*
single room	*habitació senzilla*	shower	*dutxa*
double room	*habitació doble*	toilet	*toaleta*
one person	*una persona*	balcony	*balcó*
one night	*una nit*	key	*clau*
reservation	*reservas*	lift	*ascensor*
room service	*servei d'habitació*	sea view	*vista al mar*

bank	*banc*	credit card	*carta de crèdit*
exchange office	*oficina de canvi*	exchange rate	*tant per cent*
post office	*correus*	commission	*comissió*
coin	*moneda*	charge	
banknote	*bitllet de banc*	cashier	*caixer*
cheque	*xec*	change	*camvi*
traveller's cheque	*xec de viatge*	foreign currency	*moneda estrangera*

café	*cafè*	starter	*primer plat*
pub/bar	*celler*	main course	*segón plat*
breakfast	*berenar*	dessert	*postres*
lunch	*dinar*	bill	*cuenta*
dinner	*sopar*	beer	*cervesa*
table	*mesa*	wine	*vi*
waiter	*cambrer*	water	*aigua*
waitress	*cambrera*	coffee	*café*

aeroplane	*avió*	single ticket	*senzill-a*
airport	*aeroport*	return ticket	*anar i tornar*
train	*tren*	non-smoking	*no fumar*
bus	*autobús*	car	*cotxe*
station	*estació*	petrol	*gasolina*
boat	*vaixell*	bus stop	*la parada*
port	*port*	how do I get to...?	*per anar a...?*
ticket	*bitllet*	where is...?	*on és...?*

yes	*si*	you're welcome	*de res*
no	*no*	how are you?	*com va?*
please	*per favor*	do you speak English?	*parla anglès?*
thank you	*gràcies*		
welcome	*de res*	I don't understand	*no ho entenc*
hello	*hola*		
goodbye	*adéu*	how much?	*quant es?*
good morning	*bon dia*	open	*obert*
good afternoon	*bona tarda*	closed	*tancat*
goodnight	*bona nit*	today	*avui*
excuse me	*perdoni*	tomorrow	*demà*

INDEX

accommodation 100–3
Acuàrium de Mallorca 109
Alcúdia 16
Algaida 43
Andratx 43
Aquapark 108
Arab Baths 32
Artà 45
arts and crafts shops 106–7
Auto-Safari 45, 61, 108

Badia de Palma 17
Balearic islands 7
banks 120
Banyalbufar 44, 46
Banys Àrabs 32
Banys de Sant Joan 51
bars 111
Basílica de Sant Francesc 32
beaches 53
Biniaraix 55
Binissalem 46
birdwatching 13, 53, 77, 85
black vulture 13
boat trips 121
Bóquer valley 70
Botanicactus 85
bullfighting 115
Bunyola 71
buses 121

Cabrera 7, 46
Cala Bona 48
Cala de Deià 22, 53
Cala Figuera 47
Cala Fornells 63
Cala Marçal 74
Cala Mesquida 61
Cala Millor 48, 53
Cala Mondragó 47
Cala d'Or 47
Cala Rajada 48
Cala Santanyí 47
Cala de Sant Vicenç 47
Cala Torta 45, 33
Cala Tuent 53, 78
Calvià 48–9
Camp de Mar 63
Campos 49
Ca'n Conrado 80
Ca'n Gordiola 43
Ca'n Solleric 39
Cap de Cala Figuera 17, 72–73
Cap de Formentor 13, 18
Cap Gros 70
Cap de Ses Salines 13, 85
Capdepera 50
Capocorb Vell 50
car rental 121
casino 112
Castell d'Alaró 19, 53
Castell de n'Amer 76
Castell de Bellver 20
Castell de Santueri 83
cellers 95
child safety 109

children's entertainment 108–9
Chopin, Frédéric 26
cinema 110
climate 118, 123
clothing sizes 123
coastline 7
coffee 52, 69, 99
Colònia de Sant Jordi 51
concerts 110
concessions 123
consulates 120
Costa Nord 14, 26, 51, 110
Cove de la Mare de Déu 72
Coves d'Artà 21
Coves del Drac 54
Coves dels Hams 54
craft fairs 106
cricket 53, 115
Cúber 13, 84
customs regulations 119
cycling 53

Deià 22
departure information 124
dinner shows 112
discos 112
Douglas, Michael 14, 51
Dragon Caves 54
Dragonera 7, 79
dress code 52
drinking water 69, 123
drives
    the central plain 65
    northeast 61
    the west 44
driving 118, 121

eating out 52–53, 92–99
El Mago 72
electricity 122
Els Blauets choir 23
Els Calderers 65, 90
entertainment 110–16
emergency telephone numbers
    119, 122
Ermita de Bonany 53, 55
Ermita de Sant Llorenç 78
Ermita de Sant Miquel 60
Es Baluard 33
Es Capdella 44
Estellencs 44

factoy outlets 107
famous Mallorcans 14
Felanitx 55
festivals and events 116
fincas 103
fish and seafood 97
flora 12
food and drink 68–69
football 115
Formentor 18, 53
Fornalutx 55
Fundació La Caixa 33
Fundació Pilar i Joan Miró 56

Galilea 44, 56
Gaudí, Antoni 23, 25

geography 7
'Goat Island' 46
golf 53, 113
Gorg Blau 13, 84
La Granja 44, 57
Graves, Robert 22

health 118, 123
Hidropark 108
history 10–11
horse-drawn carriage rides 108
horse-racing 115
horse riding 53
hotels 100–3

Inca 7, 58
insurance 118, 123

Jardins de Alfábia 58

language 7, 52, 124
La Llotja 33
Lluc 23
Lluc-Alcari 58
Llucmajor 59
Llull, Ramón 14, 32, 75
local ways and customs 52

Magaluf 17, 59
Manacor 7, 60
maps
    Badia de Palma 72–73
    Mallorca 28–29
    Palma City Centre 34–35
Marineland 109
Marivent 72
markets 104
Menorca, trips to 48, 121
Mercat de l'Olivar 37
mini golf 109
Mirador des Colomer 18
Mirador de Ses Animes 44, 53
Mirador de Ses Barques 53
Miramar 88
Miró, Joan 14, 38, 56, 106
monastery accommodation 102
money 119
Montuïri 60
mountains 7
Muro 62, 65
Museu d'Art Espanyol
    Contemporani 37
Museu de Sóller 87
Museu Etnòlogic de Mallorca 62
Museu de Mallorca 37
Museu Monogràfic de Pollentia
    16
museums 120

national holidays 120
Natura Parc 80, 109
Natural Science Museum 87
Nemo Submarines 109

olives 98
opening hours 105, 120
Oratori de Nostra Senyora de
    Gràcia 75

Acknowledgements

The Automobile Assocation wishes to thank the following photographers, libraries and
associations for their assistance in the preparation of this book:
BRIDGEMAN ART LIBRARY 56 La Vent Parmi Les Roseaux, 1971, by Joan Miró (Marlborough
Graphics, London); MARY EVANS PICTURE LIBRARY 11, 14b; NATURE PHOTOGRAPHERS 13
(Kevin Carlson); SPECTRUM COLOUR LIBRARY 7, 17, 20, 24/5, 26, 48, 58/9, 63;
www.euro.ecb.int/ 119 (euro notes).

The remaining photographs are held in the Association's own library (AA PHOTO LIBRARY) and
were taken by P BAKER, except: H RAINBOW 75, 76, 85; J A TIMS 122a; W VOYSEY 9a, 15a,
27b, 35, 67, 79, 80, 91b.

Contributors
Revision Management: Apostrophe S Ltd Page Layout: Design 23 Indexer: Marie Lorimer

Dear Essential Traveller

**Your comments, opinions and recommendations are very
important to us. So please help us to improve our travel
guides by taking a few minutes to complete this simple
questionnaire.**

*You do not need a stamp (unless posted outside the UK). If you do not want to cut this page
from your guide, then photocopy it or write your answers on a plain sheet of paper.*

Send to: **The Editor, AA World Travel Guides,
FREEPOST SCE 4598, Basingstoke RG21 4GY.**

Your recommendations...

We always encourage readers' recommendations for restaurants, nightlife
or shopping – if your recommendation is used in the next edition of the
guide, we will send you a *FREE* **AA** *Essential* **Guide** of your choice.
Please state below the establishment name, location and your reasons
for recommending it.

_____
_____
_____
_____

Please send me **AA** *Essential* _____

About this guide...

Which title did you buy?
    AA *Essential* _____
Where did you buy it? _____
When? m m / y y

Why did you choose an AA *Essential* Guide? _____

_____
_____
_____
_____

Did this guide meet your expectations?
    Exceeded ☐ Met all ☐ Met most ☐ Fell below ☐
    Please give your reasons _____

_____
_____
_____

continued on next page...

Were there any aspects of this guide that you particularly liked? _____

_____

_____

Is there anything we could have done better? _____

_____

_____

About you...

Name (*Mr/Mrs/Ms*) _____

    Address _____

_____

    _____ Postcode _____

Daytime tel nos _____

Please only give us your mobile phone number if you wish to hear from us
about other products and services from the AA and partners by text or mms.

Which age group are you in?
    Under 25 ☐   25–34 ☐   35–44 ☐   45–54 ☐   55–64 ☐   65+ ☐

How many trips do you make a year?
    Less than one ☐   One ☐   Two ☐   Three or more ☐

Are you an AA member? Yes ☐   No ☐

About your trip...

When did you book? m m / y y   When did you travel? m m / y y
How long did you stay? _____
Was it for business or leisure? _____
Did you buy any other travel guides for your trip?
    If yes, which ones? _____

Thank you for taking the time to complete this questionnaire. Please send it to us as soon as
possible, and remember, you do not need a stamp (*unless posted outside the UK*).

Happy Holidays!

The Atlas

Acknowledgements
All pictures are from AA World Travel Library with contributions from the following photographers:
Jainie Cowham: waterfront scene
Ken Paterson: night time in Pollença, tourist train, underground caves, evening entertainment

Day One

Day Two

Day Three

Day Four

Day Five

Day Six

Day Seven

The Automobile Association
www.theAA.com
The Automobile Association's website offers comprehensive and up-to-the-minute information on insurance, European motoring advice, AA-approved hotels, B&Bs, restaurants and pubs, along with the latest traffic information, detailed UK routes, airport parking, a bookshop and much more.

The Foreign and Commonwealth Office
Country advice, traveller's tips, before you go information, checklists and more.
www.fco.gov.uk

Spanish National Tourist Office
www.tourspain.co.uk
Online brochure ordering service.

GENERAL
UK Passport Service
www.ukpa.gov.uk

Health Advice for Travellers
www.doh.gov.uk/traveladvice

UK Travel Insurance Directory
www.uktravelinsurancedirectory.co.uk

BBC – Holiday
www.bbc.co.uk/holiday

The Full Universal Currency Converter
www.xe.com/ucc/full.shtml

Flying with Kids
www.flyingwithkids.com

What to see, towns to visit, excursions, beaches and nightlife.
www.red2000.com

Events, shopping, beaches, walking, watersports
www.puertopollensa.com

Useful information on all the main resorts
www.majorca-mallorca.co.uk

TRAVEL
Flights and Information
www.cheapflights.co.uk
www.thisistravel.co.uk
www.ba.com
www.worldairportguide.com

Motorway · Toll junction · Toll station · Junction with number · Motel · Restaurant · Snack bar · Filling station · Parking place with and without WC	Trento 11	Autobahn · Gebührenpflichtige Anschlussstelle · Gebührenstelle · Anschlussstelle mit Nummer · Rasthaus mit Übernachtung · Raststätte · Kleinraststätte · Tankstelle · Parkplatz mit und ohne WC
Motorway under construction and projected with completion date	Date Datum	Autobahn in Bau und geplant mit Datum der Verkehrsübergabe
Dual carriageway (4 lanes)		Zweibahnige Straße (4-spurig)
Trunk road · Road numbers	14 E45	Fernverkehrsstraße · Straßennummern
Important main road		Wichtige Hauptstraße
Main road · Tunnel · Bridge	)=(	Hauptstraße · Tunnel · Brücke
Minor roads		Nebenstraßen
Track · Footpath		Fahrweg · Fußweg
Tourist footpath (selection)	– – – – –	Wanderweg (Auswahl)
Main line railway		Eisenbahn mit Fernverkehr
Rack railway, funicular		Zahnradbahn, Standseilbahn
Aerial cableway · Chair lift	o—o—o o++++++o	Kabinenschwebebahn · Sessellift
Car ferry	•———	Autofähre
Nature reserve · Prohibited area		Naturschutzgebiet · Sperrgebiet
National park, natural park · Forest		Nationalpark, Naturpark · Wald
Tourist route · Pass	Weinstraße ^1510	Touristenstraße · Pass
Scenic view · Panoramic view · Route with beautiful scenery		Schöner Ausblick · Rundblick · Landschaftlich bes. schöne Strecke
International airport		Internationaler Flughafen
Spa · Swimming pool		Heilbad · Schwimmbad
Youth hostel · Camping site		Jugendherberge · Campingplatz
Golf course · Ski jump		Golfplatz · Sprungschanze
Church · Chapel		Kirche im Ort, freistehend · Kapelle
Monastery · Monastery ruin		Kloster · Klosterruine
Palace, castle · Ruin		Schloss, Burg · Schloss-, Burgruine
Tower · Radio-, TV-tower		Turm · Funk-, Fernsehturm
Lighthouse · Power station		Leuchtturm · Kraftwerk
Waterfall · Lock		Wasserfall · Schleuse
Important building · Market place, area		Bauwerk · Marktplatz, Areal
Arch excavation, ruins · Mine		Ausgrabungs- u. Ruinenstätte · Bergwerk
Dolmen · Menhir · Nuraghe		Dolmen · Menhir · Nuraghen
Cairn · Military cemetery		Hünen-, Hügelgrab · Soldatenfriedhof
Hotel, inn, refuge · Cave		Hotel, Gasthaus, Berghütte · Höhle

Culture		**Kultur**
Picturesque town · Elevation	WIEN (171)	Malerisches Ortsbild · Ortshöhe
Worth a journey	★★ MILANO	Eine Reise wert
Worth a detour	★ TEMPLIN	Lohnt einen Umweg
Worth seeing	Andermatt	Sehenswert
Landscape Worth a journey	★★ Las Cañadas	**Landschaft** Eine Reise wert
Worth a detour	★ Texel	Lohnt einen Umweg
Worth seeing	Dikti	Sehenswert

```
0        4        8 km
0        2        4 miles
```

Maps © Mairs Geographischer Verlag / Falk Verlag, 73751 Ostfildern

135

	D	E	F

1

Punta Topina   Punta Galera
Punta Beca   Punta Extrema   Punta de
Cala de Sant   Covas Blancas
Cornavacas   Vicenç

Cova de Sas Cabras   Punta   Cast. del Rei
Punta de la Sal   544   Cala de
Cala Sollerich   Sant Vincente   Los
Figueretes   Ternellas   Sa Celda   Enginares   Port de Pollença
Torre de Ariant   838   220-3   el Vilà
os de ses Cordes   Ternellas   Estrecho   Gotmars
634   de Ternellas   PM-220   **2**
389   Masot   Torrent   de   Ternella
389   Pont Roma   1,5   Sant   Camp de Mar
798   Puig de Calvari   esglesia de Templer   Jordi
Caragoler   Mortitxet   **20**   ermita de   Ermita de la Mare   5   **15**
20   395   C710   Roservell   de Deu del Puig   92
Femenies   **Pollença**   Son Brull
Vell   le Vall d'en Marc   Puig de Maria   Almadraba   Albufereta   **3**
Montana   Serra de sa Coma   Son Ferra   6,5
13,5   es Rafal   4,5
Tomir   Puig d'es Ca   Serra   de   Son   Axartell   Can
Son   885   442
Alzines   Binifaldo   1102
825   Pas d'en Bisquerra   **12**   **12**
Sa Moleta   Rafal de Casellas   334   Font de   Ermita
nestició de Lluc   PM-220   Mina de Son Fé
753   Binatro?   Co de Son Vila   266   **4**
Puig Ferret   Fangar   323   C713   Puig de Son Fé
190   Sant Miquel   Cretaix   4,5
4,5   Libelli Gran   Puig d'es Fangar   Can
PM-213   Sant Miquel   Coves de Campanet   a Punta des Vent
Barracar   Mannaber   Sqd Cladera   2,6   3,5
es Barraca   Nou   343-3
Finca es Castell   Santiani   PM-342   Huerta   de
621   Binibona   **16**   5   Ullaro   La Puebla
5,5   **Campanet**   342-1   **5**
mari   134   sa Pobla   La Puebla
213-2   Vin Roma
Selva   213-1   **Búger**   4,5
all   3   Moscaci   **13**
1,5   Torrent   sa Canova   Museu de
C713   Son Vivet   Ermita de   PM-350   Mallorca
Puig   Ermita   Sant Vincenc   3,5
Inca   de Inca   Santa   **Muro**
Santa Maria   Magdalena   173
PM-344   Serra de   Son Mulet   PM-343
Santa Magdalena   PM-344   **6**
Hostal   304   2,5
d'es Bru   Ermita   2,5
M-27   5,5   Remei
PM-312   **Llubí**
Son Llusia   es Jornets   s'Hort   3,5
den Bordils

137	143

This is a full-page map (page 143) showing part of Mallorca, including the following labelled places and features:

Towns and villages:
- Campanet
- sa Pobla
- La Puebla
- Huerta de
- Muro
- Búger
- Ullaró
- Moscari
- Puig de Inca
- Inca
- Santa Maria
- Llubí
- Maria de la Salut
- Sencelles
- Sineu
- Costitx
- Lloret de Vista Alegre
- Sant Joan
- Pina
- Son Mezquida Nou
- Montuïri
- Algaida
- Porreres
- Randa
- Castellitx
- Aubenya

Roads:
- C713
- PM-342
- PM-343
- PM-344
- PM-350
- PM-351
- PM-312
- PM-313
- PM-314
- PM-322
- PM-323
- PM-324
- PM-330
- PM-503
- 330-1
- 342-1
- 343-3
- 213-1
- 213-2
- 311-1
- 510-1
- 501-8
- C715

Other features / labels:
- Cretaix
- Fangar
- Puig d'es Fangar
- Sant Miquel
- Coves de Campanet
- Llibelli Gran
- Mannaber
- Finca Es Castell Santjani
- Binibona
- Barraca
- es Barraca
- Son Pol
- sa Punta des Vent
- Son Cladera
- Son Pa
- Son Vivot
- Vin Roma
- Museu de Mallorca
- Ermita Santa Magdalena (299)
- Serra de Santa Magdalena 304
- sa Canova
- Ermita de Sant Vinicenc
- Son Mulet
- Ermita Remei (73)
- Hostal p. esserra
- Son Llusia
- es Jornets
- s'Hort d'en Bordils
- Son Aloy
- sa Font
- Talaiot de Son Fred
- Museu (185)
- Cas Canar
- Son Binifart
- Ruberts
- Benasque
- Santuari de la Concepción (144)
- Mare de Deu del Angels
- Defla
- Estanqueta de Buix
- sa Torre
- sa Samentera
- Son Rex
- Son Brondo
- sa Bastida
- Son Malmü
- Son Cervera
- Son Molt
- Son Clubi
- Company
- Son Tagamanent
- Can Miquel Ribas
- Casucha
- Santuari de la Consolacio
- es Calderes
- Son Gil
- Can Xota
- Son Gat
- Son Mezquida Nou
- Son Mayol
- Son Palou
- Son Ribas
- Son Comellas
- Ermita Sant Miquel
- Hortella Vey
- es Pagos
- Son Valent
- Puig de Randa
- Santuari de la Mare de Deu de Cura
- Santuari de Sant Honorat
- sa Maimona
- Ermita de la Pau, Coll Vey
- Ermita de Santa Creu
- Can Arnau
- 137
- 149
- 143
- 200

Numerous distance numbers appear along the roads: 2.5, 2, 3, 4.5, 1.5, 3.5, 5, 6.5, 8.5, 7.5, 5.5, 7, 9.5, 6, 8, etc.

Grid references: D, E, F, S, 1, 2, 3, 4, 5, 6, 13, 16, 34, 18

Sart de Valldemossa

D 874 ★ Son Morague Binifarell Nou Jardins **E** Alfabia Coll de Hono **F** s'Aveno de Son Pou

★ **Valldemossa** (425) Binifaranl Vey Alfabia 11

Cartoixa de Valldemossa sa Coma 8 ★★★ sa Alqueria ▲ 141 Casa Garraguer Son Pou **1**

C710 8 714 Son Ferrandel PM-111 650 Fatima T **Bunyola** 233 Namariet 666 Es Cabas

Nova Valldemossa Boxos 626 7 19 Son Puig ★ Raixa 203 PM-202 Es Cabas

Son Cabaspre 593 Cabaspre Son Patx Son Termens Sanatorio Juan March 203-2 ① PM-202

Esporles (196) Son Quint Son Masellas PM-203 Can Roig Son Vivot 1 1.5

Son Miralles PM-114 **Palmanyola** 3.5 Son Rafalet Can Arbona Son Sureda Marratxi

PM-112 Sement 307 4.5 Son Canet s'Esglaieta Son Figuerola Can d'loca es Cañulls Marratxi Sa Cabaneta

PM-104 Can Canet Sa Cabana 203-1 PM-204 Santa María sa Cabaneta

Sarria Cas Font Son Bibilont Cas Tixado Nou els Garrofets Can Farineta sa Cabaneta

Establiments Nous Cas Metje PM-111 4.5 Can Verl ② **Marratxi**

Can Amorós 2.5 Pureza 2.5 Son Sardina Cap C713 Villa Mogreal Partof **3**

font Alma Son Gual Son Berða la Victoria Es Font d'Inca PM-27

Establiments Bella Vista Surat Ses Figeral la Real 1.5 la Indiomeria Coronell 1.5 Oas Capitá se Plsta

Cans Puig d'es Bons Son Anglada la Real Salfar Estació Pia d'Inca ⊕ 12 301-7

885 Son Roca Valldemossa Font d'Inca 10 Rafal 1.5 Creu Vermella 11

sa Vileta Inca PM-20 d'Alc Creu Vermella

PALMA ★★★ Pizza Sa Vileta ☨ LA SOLEDAD 301-1 Son Ferriol C715 2.5

DE MALLORCA (33) Castell de LA SOLEDAD San Marcos PM-301 Son Banya Aeropuerto Palma de Mallorca 501-3

Génova Bellver EL TERRENO 3 Cala Portixol PM-19 4 Son Banya ✈ **4**

Gruta de Génova Coll d'En Rabassa 5 4

nova Sant Agustí Cala Major **EL MOLINAR** Ciudad Jardin Coll d'en Rabassa Aeroport/Can Pastilla

PM-1 Sant Agustí Fund. Platja Ciudad Jardin Cala Gamba Pl. de Palma/Can Pastill Sant Manacor **5**

12 Cas Catala P. J. Mirò Torre de Pelaires Porto Cala Estancia Can Pastilla I. GALERA Francesc

Nous 4.5 ses Illetes I. de la CALETA Platja d'Illetes Cala Estancia Platja de Palma **11**

SALAS I. des PAS Platja de Palma las Maravillas **12**

Playa de s'Arenal las Cadenas Las Canta

Badia de Palma s'Arenal Aquacity Son Veri **5**

rrassa Cala Blava Cala Blava

Cap Enderrocat 2 Bella Vista

3.5 ses Palmeres 601-4 Son Granad d'Abai

es Puntarró Punta Negra Cala Vella ses Olles la Moreria **6**

many 4½ h. ssa, Ibiza 2½–4½ h. Mao (Menorca) 6½ h. sa Torre Badia

▲ **147** ▼ **148** Casetes Badia Blava Marsals badia Grande

D

Coves dels Hams

Son Móro

Portocristo

Cala Manacor

401-4

Portocristo Nova

Coves del Drac ★ ★

Cala Anguila

Punta Reina

Cala Estany

Romanica

Pirata

Fronton d'es Mula

Cala Falcó

Cala Varques

Punta d'es Llevants

Cala Serrat

Pilar **Coves del Pilar**

Cala Magraner

Cala Virgili

ala Bota

la Saldat

a Setrill

Antena

aguera

Domingos

Murada

Algar

le ses Crestes

one

E

Cala Petita

F

▲ 145

1

2

Calas de Mallorca

3

M A R.

4

M E D I T E R R À N I A

5

6

Sight Locator Index

This index relates to the atlas section on pages 136–51. We have given map references to the main sights of interest in the book. Some sights in the index may not be plotted on the atlas. **Note: ibc – inside back cover.**

For the main index see pages 125–26